THE BULLS OF FRANCISCO DE GOYA

75 masterpieces

José René Cruz Revueltas

Idbcom LLC

Copyright © 2022 Idbcom LLC

All rights reserved

The characters and events portrayed in this book are fictitious. Any similarity to real persons, living or dead, is coincidental and not intended by the author.

No part of this book may be reproduced, or stored in a retrieval system, or transmitted in any form or by any means, electronic, mechanical, photocopying, recording, or otherwise, without express written permission of the publisher.

ISBN-13: 9798831265552

All images are in the public domain
Cover design by: Idbcom LLC
Library of Congress Control Number: 2018675309
Printed in the United States of America

Having to proceed against painters in accordance with rule 11 of the expurgation procedure, and given that Don Francisco de Goya is the author of two of the works ['La maja desnuda' and the 'La maja vestida'].. ..one of them representing a naked woman on a bed.. ..and the other a women dressed as a 'maja' on a bed.. ..the said Goya [should] be ordered to appear before this tribunal so as to identify them and state whether they are his work, for what reasons he did them, at whose request and what intention guided him.

QUOTE IN A COURT INQUISITION DOCUMENT OF 1815, WRITTEN BY DR. ZORILLA DE VELASCO, MEMBER OF THE SECRET CHAMBER OF COURT INQUISITION

CONTENTS

Title Page
Copyright
Epigraph
Introduction
Self portraits   1
Manolas y majas   9
Bullfighters   15
Bull fighting   18
La Tauromaquia   32
Bordeaux   74
Others   79
Catalog of Idbcom Publishing   83
Books In This Series   85

INTRODUCTION

Goya was always, in addition to being a painter, a Spaniard, and fundamentally an Aragonese. He never despised his birthplace or his origin but rather showed, through his art, his knowledge of Spanish customs and traditions. His passion was Spain: his land, sun, and love. Goya could not banish his fondness for good wine, bulls, and women from his heart.

Bullfighting, art as Spanish as Spain itself, and Goyesque as Goya himself: Light, beauty, aesthetics, and the possibility of a grotesque death in a sadomasochistic act transform joy into anguish, beauty into horror, and life in pain and death.

The bulls are the Spanish national festival that could define Goya and Spain itself.

Spain was born from the triumph of absolutist Christianity over the Moors and the Jews. That grows with the wealth of its colonies. But with the establishment of the holy inquisition, he condemns his people to live under terror and suspicion. Wherever there is a desire and transgression, no matter how small, there is sin and the possibility of brutal punishment in this life or Hell.

Spain that after its initial greatness, consumes itself. And that by the time of Goya, it had become the Spain of Don Quixote, of Lazarillo de Tormes, of the Buscón de Quevedo. When the good years were behind, the people had to defend themselves with their ingenuity to survive and dream in a challenging social context.

And it is in the festival of the bull where the Spanish people find a catharsis against that unequal, unjust, corrupt world where the decadent court lives in luxury, deceit, and lies.

There can be no lies in the bulls. Courage and bravery cannot be hidden. Beauty, art, and bravery are confronted as equals with the most real truths we know: fear, pain, and death.

Goya was famous for his drunkenness, love affairs with maidens and married women, and a distinctive sign of his character, his fondness for bullfighting. He often signed his letters as "Francisco, the one with the bulls."

As a young man, Goya tried to apply for a fellowship at the Royal Academy of Arts in Madrid, twice being turned down. Before him, there was room for those recommended from the larger provinces, mainly Andalusians and Castilians. And he, being an Aragonese with no influence at court, a stranger without work, a hillbilly and ignorant, despite his solid national roots, could not obtain any position. So, to survive, he secured a certain amount of money by fighting bulls in provincial arenas.

Now in his eighties, Goya continued to flaunt his erudition in matters of bullfighting, bullfighters, and bullrings. He also boasted that he could still give the most colorful bull passes, much of his temperament and personality.

In the following pages, you will be able to observe the series of La Tauromaquia that consists of 33 engravings that Francisco de Goya published in 1816. These works were elaborated slowly, without a specific plan. You will also appreciate the results of the "Bulls of Bordeaux" series painted between 1824 and 1825 in the French city of Bordeaux.

Unlike "La Tauromaquia", these works reflect professional bullfights and the sets of well-known bullfighters. Together with the bullfighters, the collective brutalization of the masses is reflected. There are also several works by Goya where the theme is bullfighting.

SELF PORTRAITS

JOSÉ RENÉ CRUZ REVUELTAS

1795

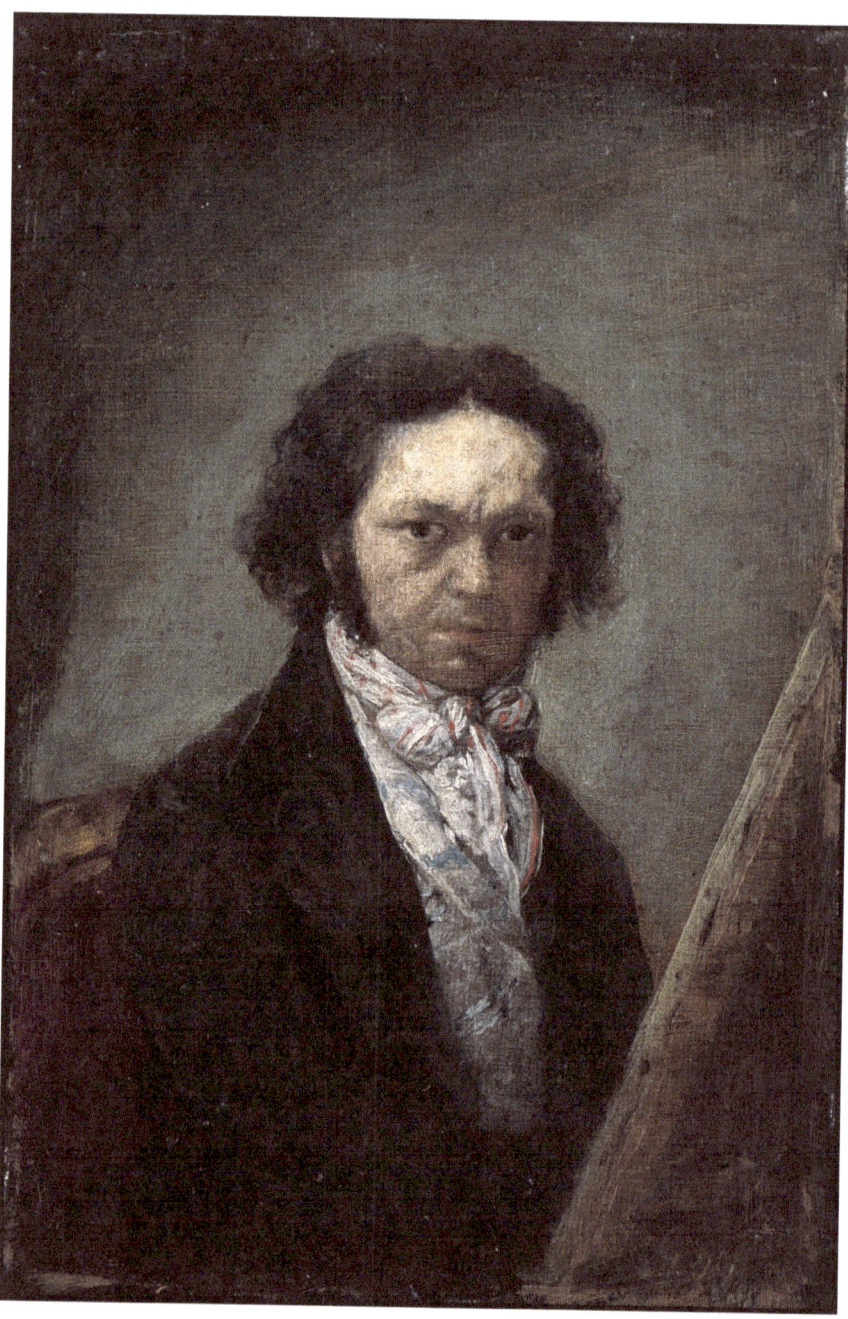

1795

In The Workshop

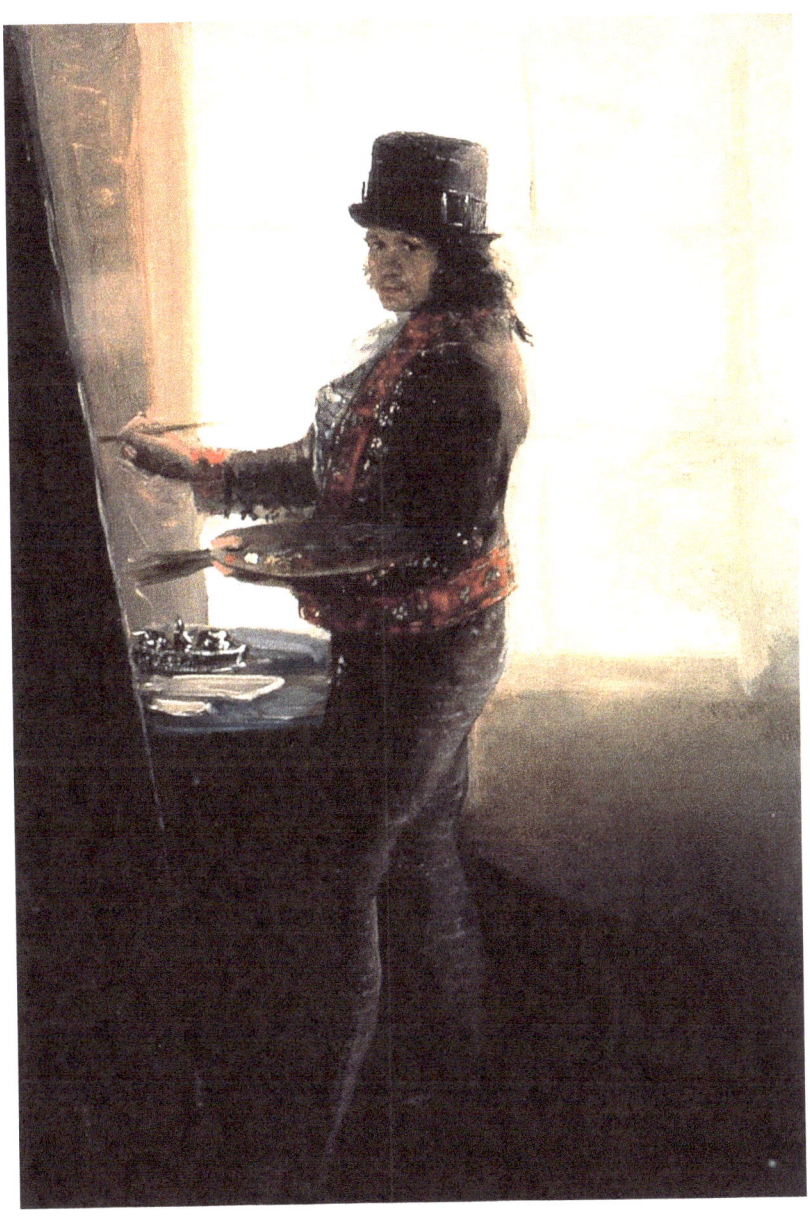

JOSÉ RENÉ CRUZ REVUELTAS

1783

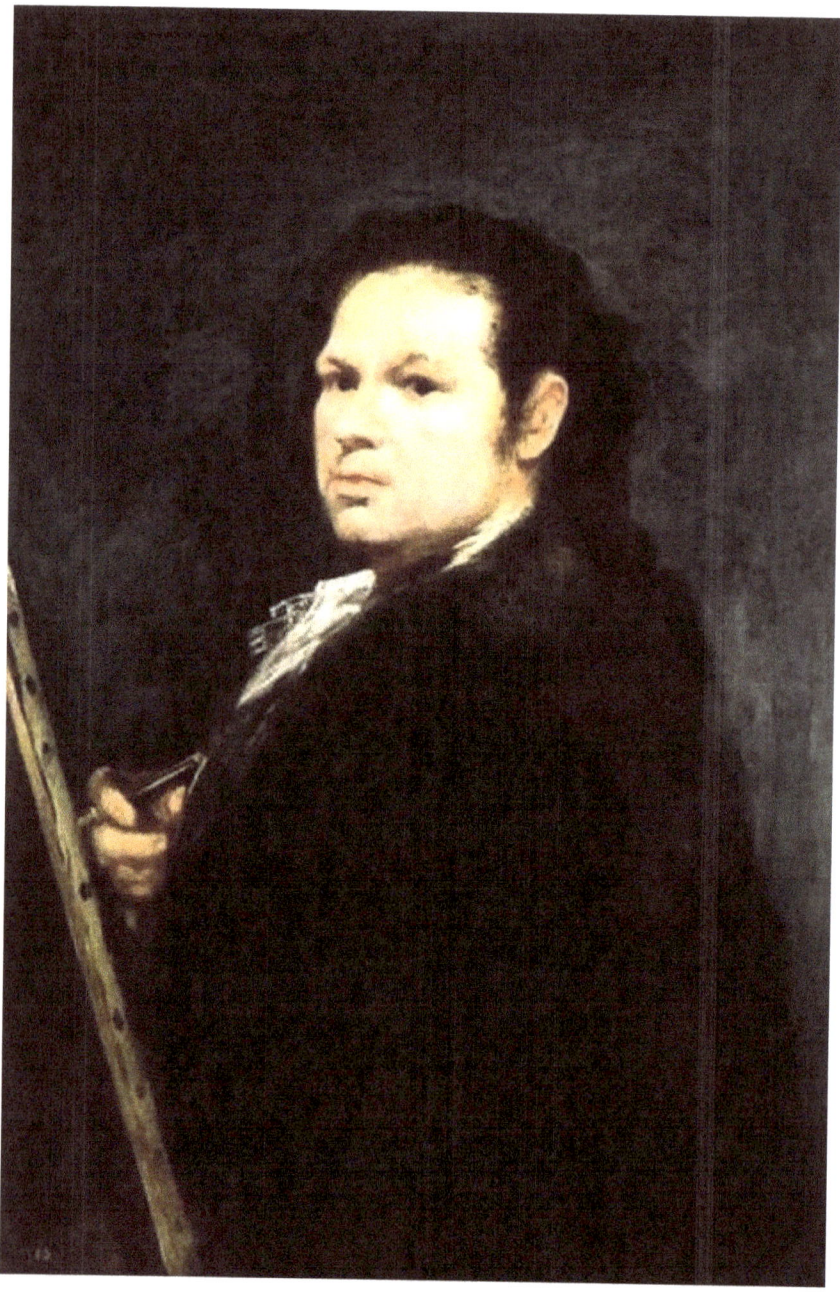

1797

1.

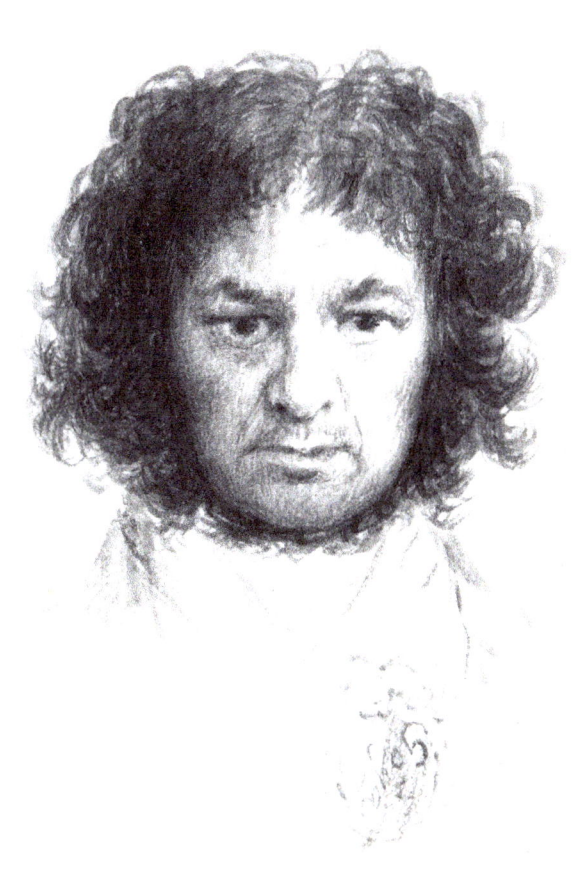

JOSÉ RENÉ CRUZ REVUELTAS

1800

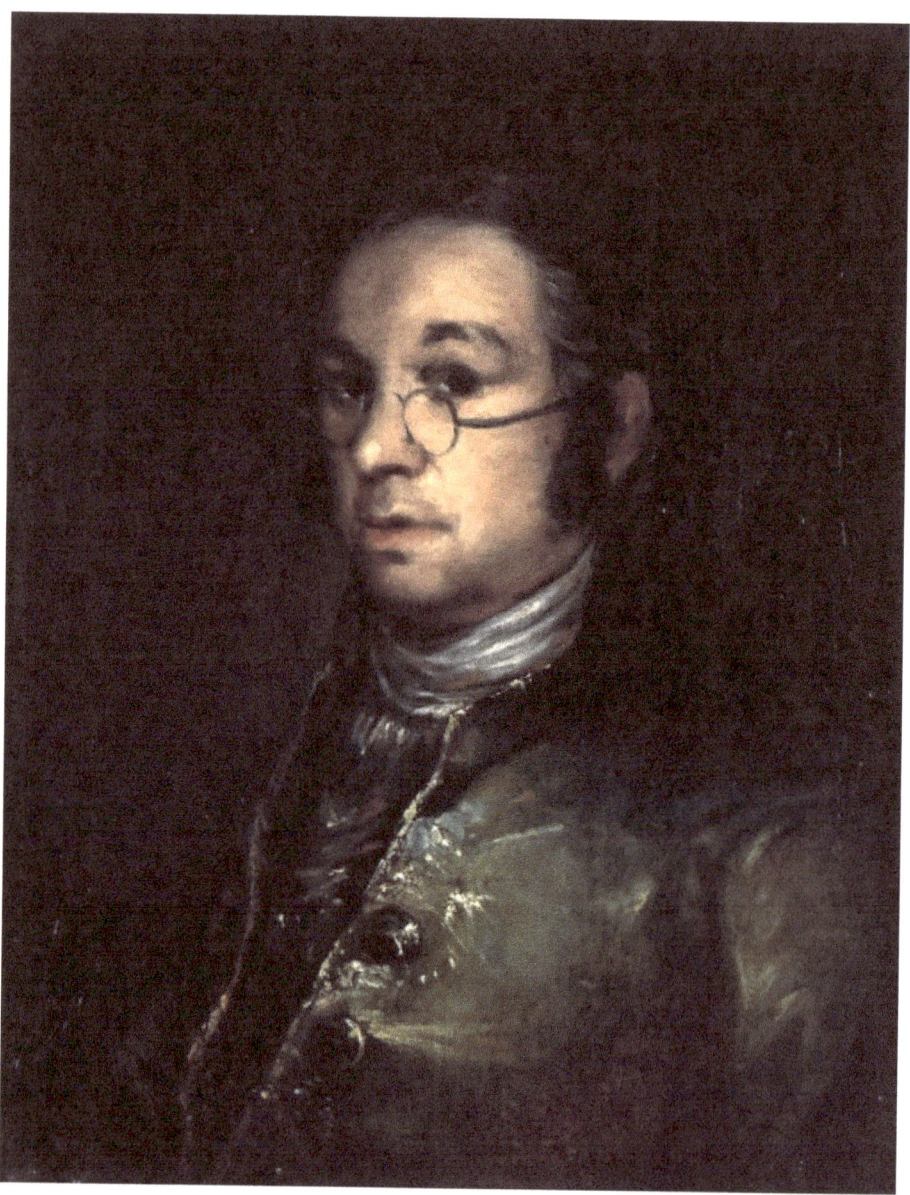

1815

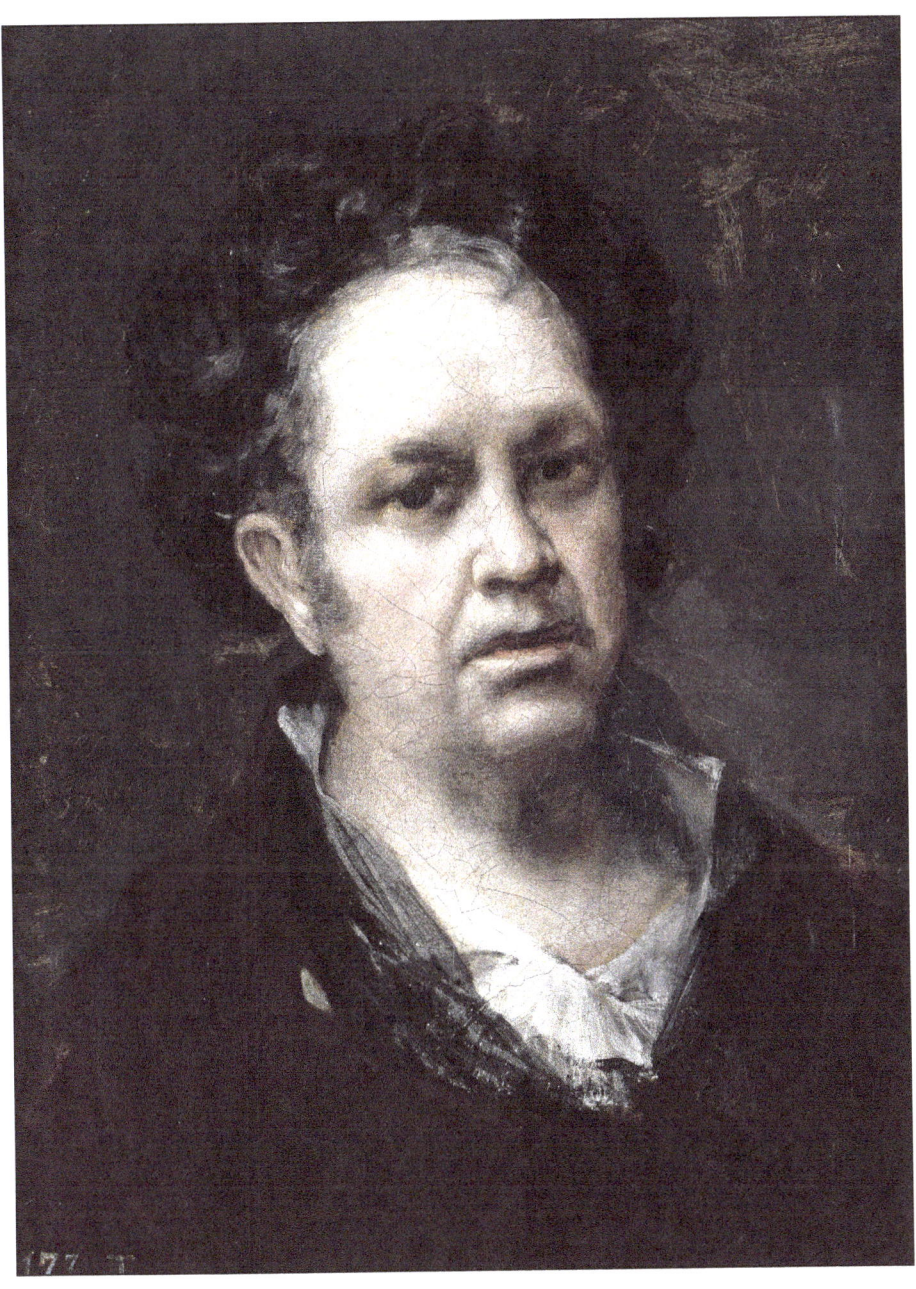

1815

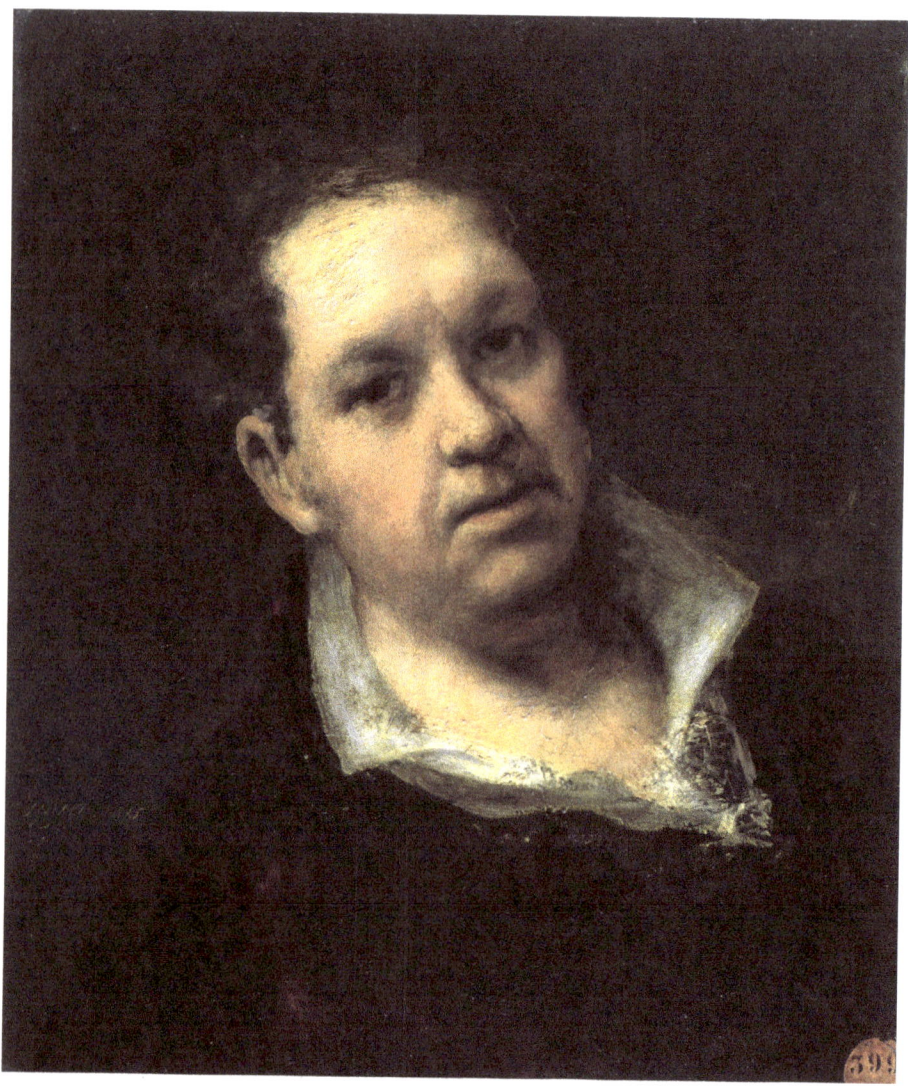

MANOLAS Y MAJAS

"La Solana" (1795)

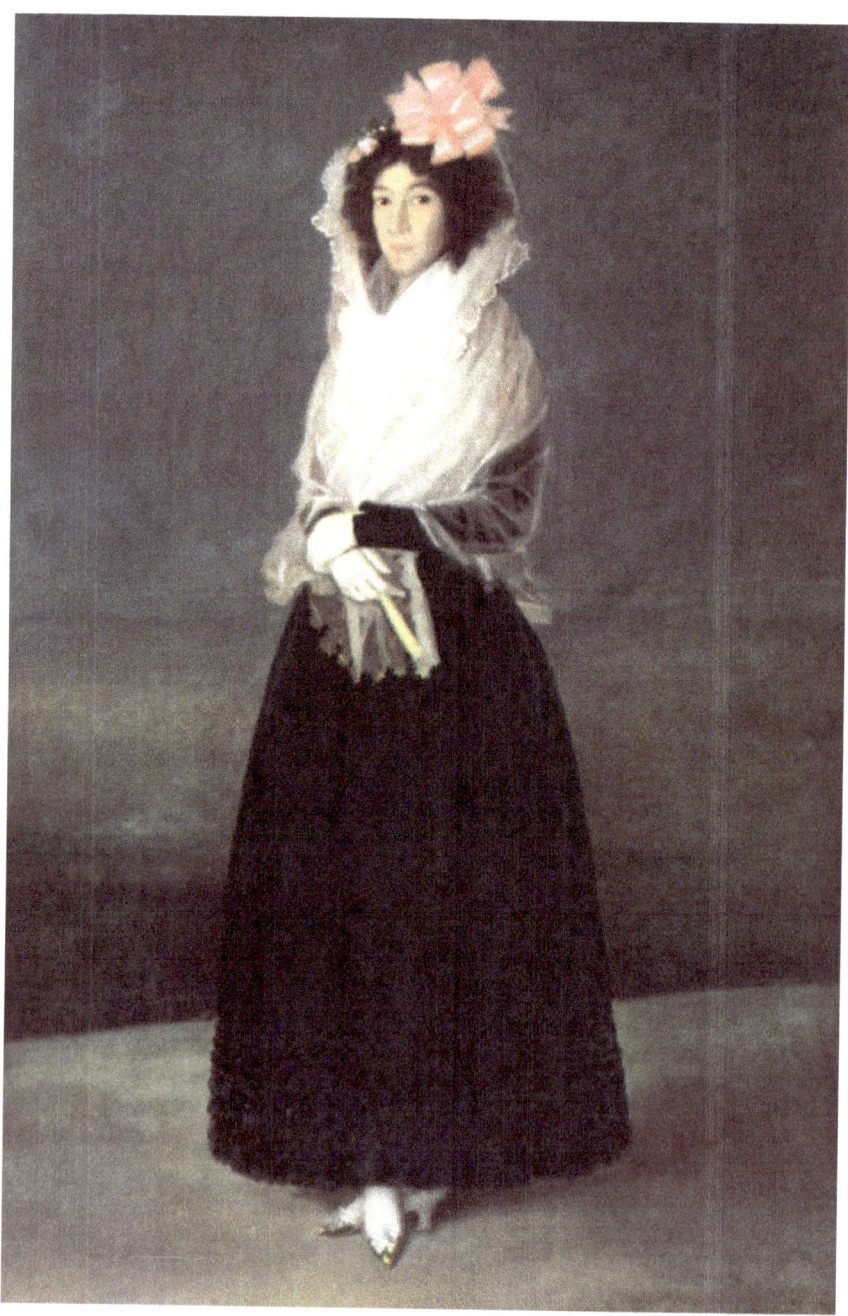

The naked maja (1800)

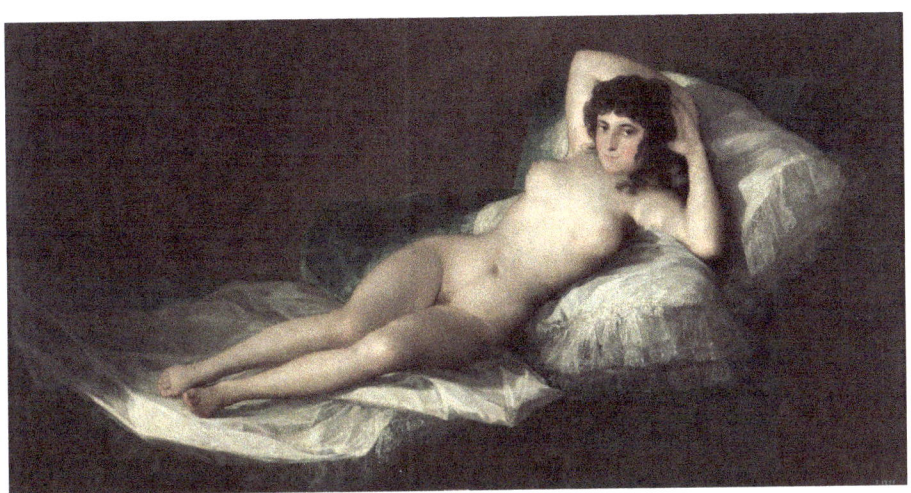

Marchioness of Santiago (1804)

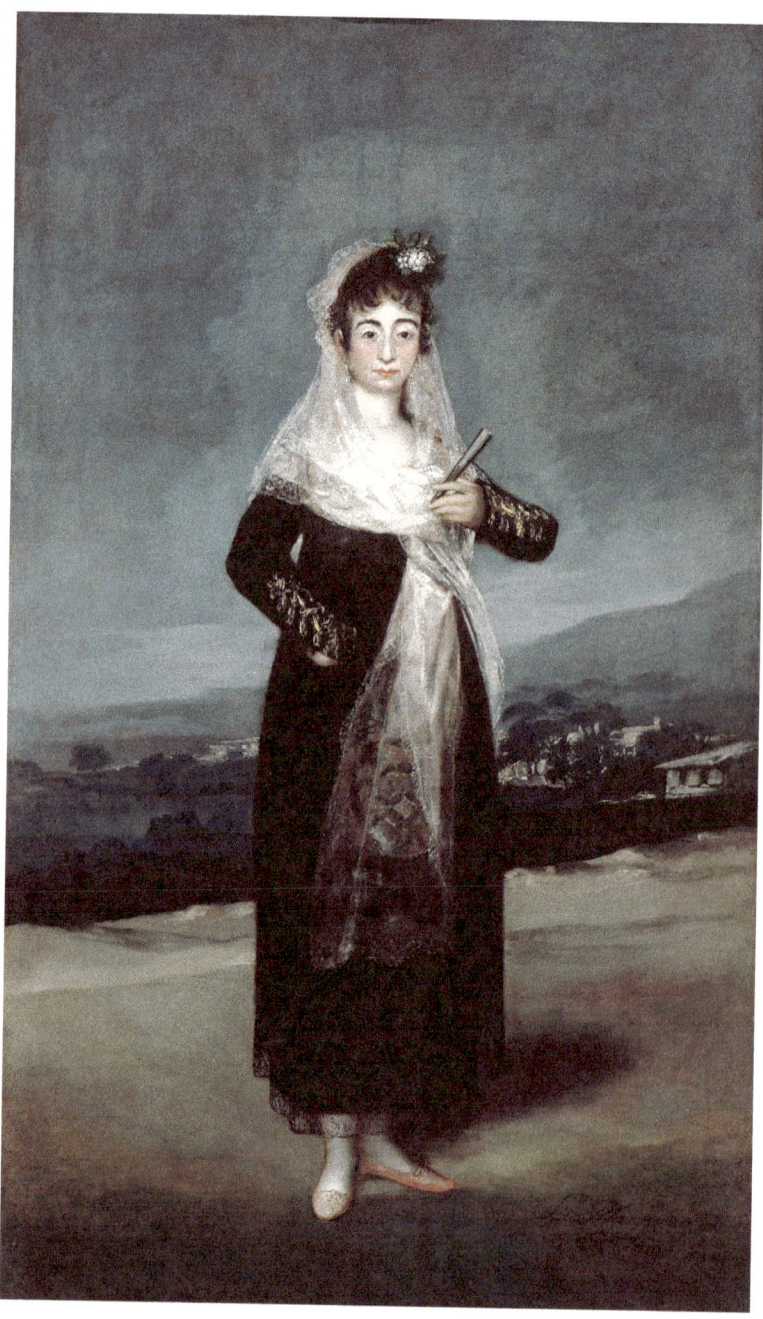

La maja vestida (1805)

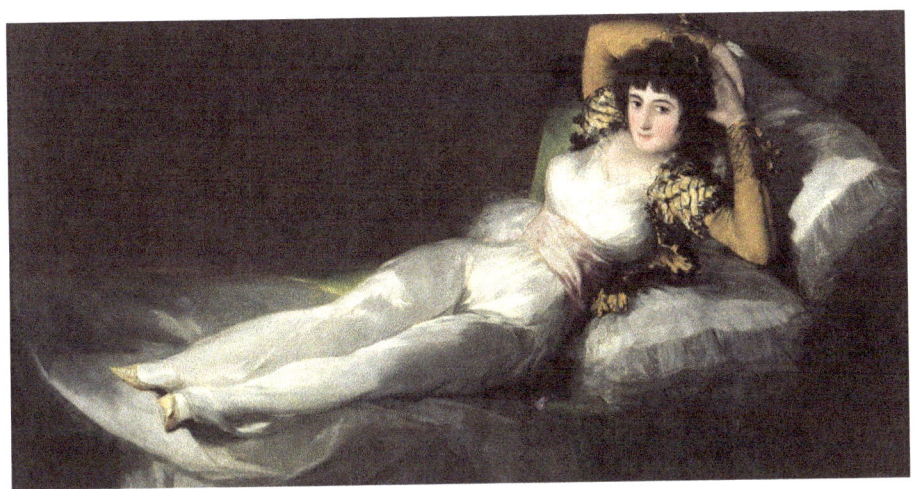

Majas to the balcony (1812)

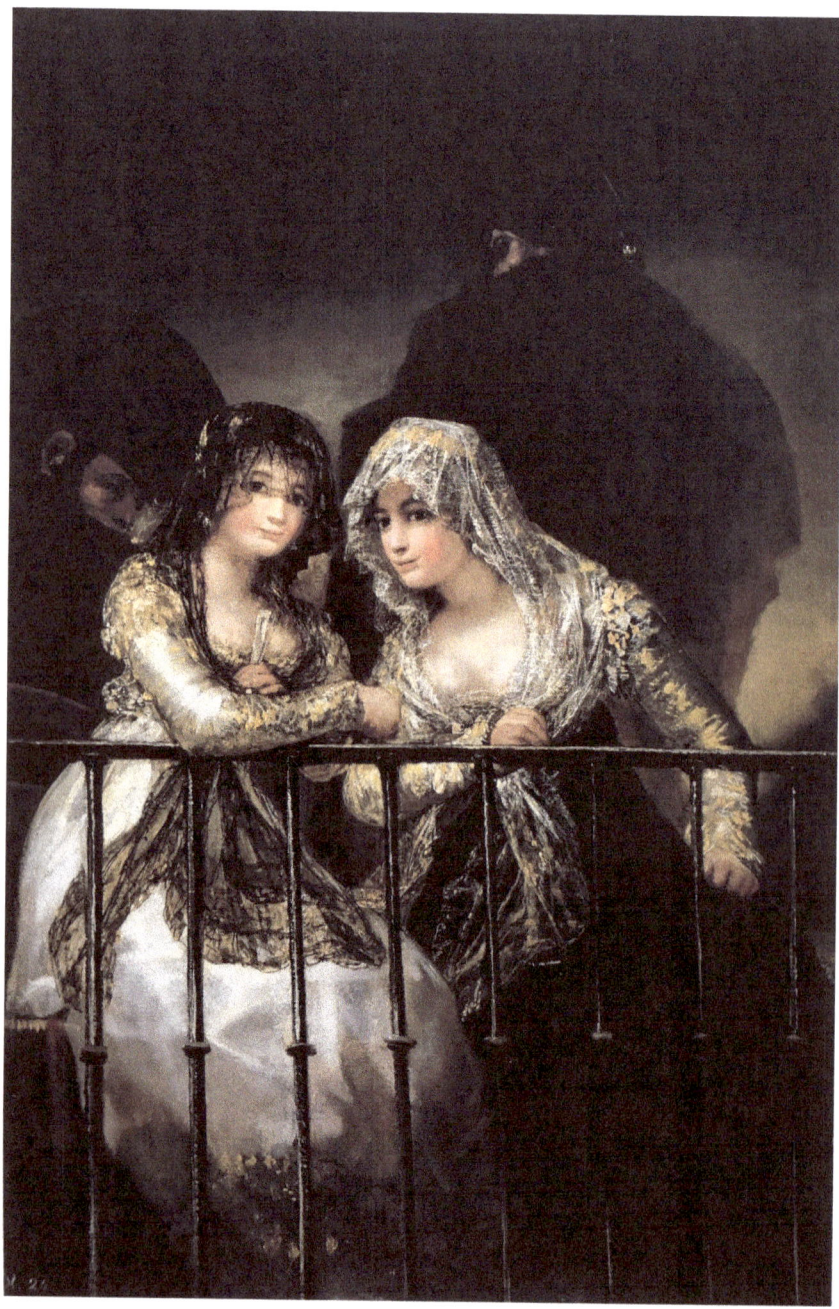

BULLFIGHTERS

Pedro Romero (1798)

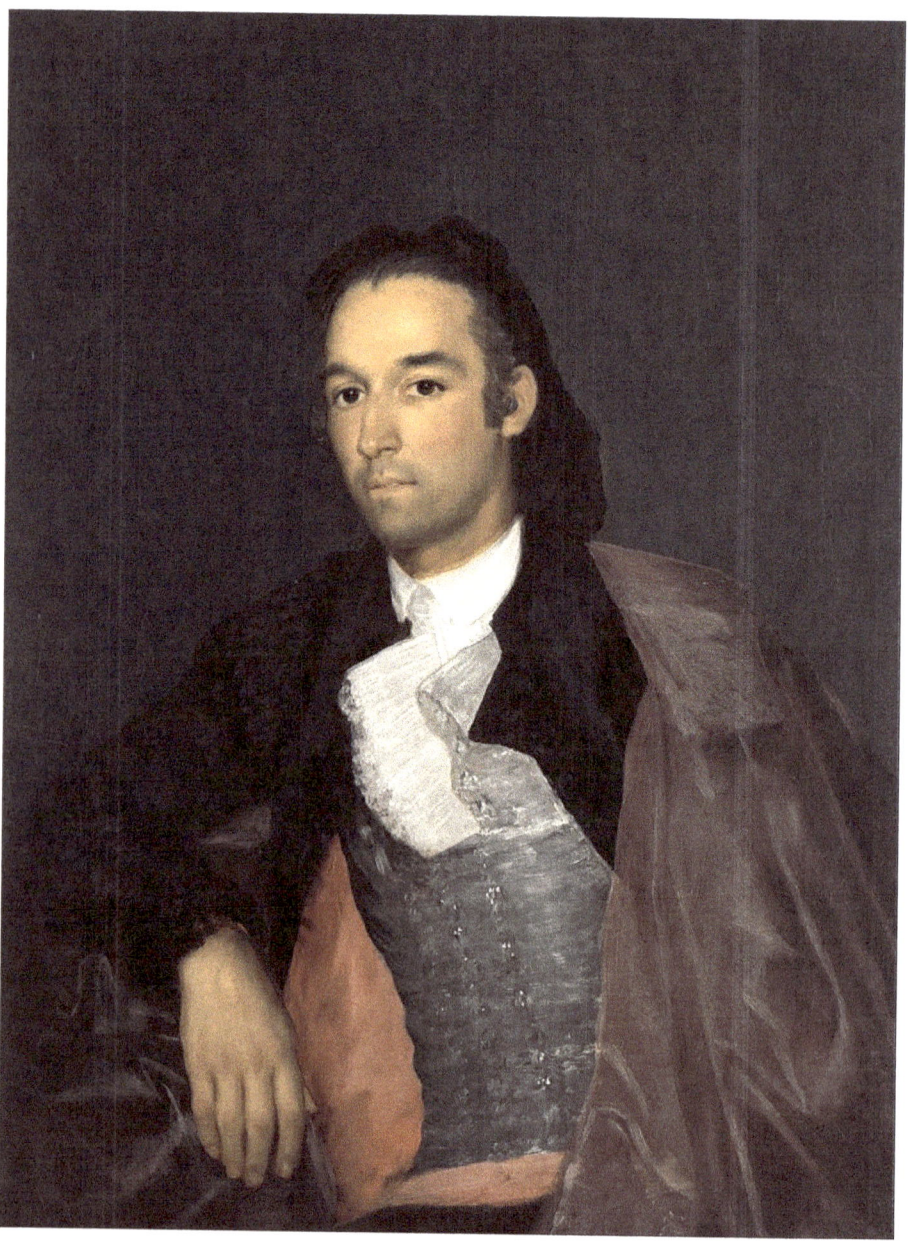

Jose Romero (1798)

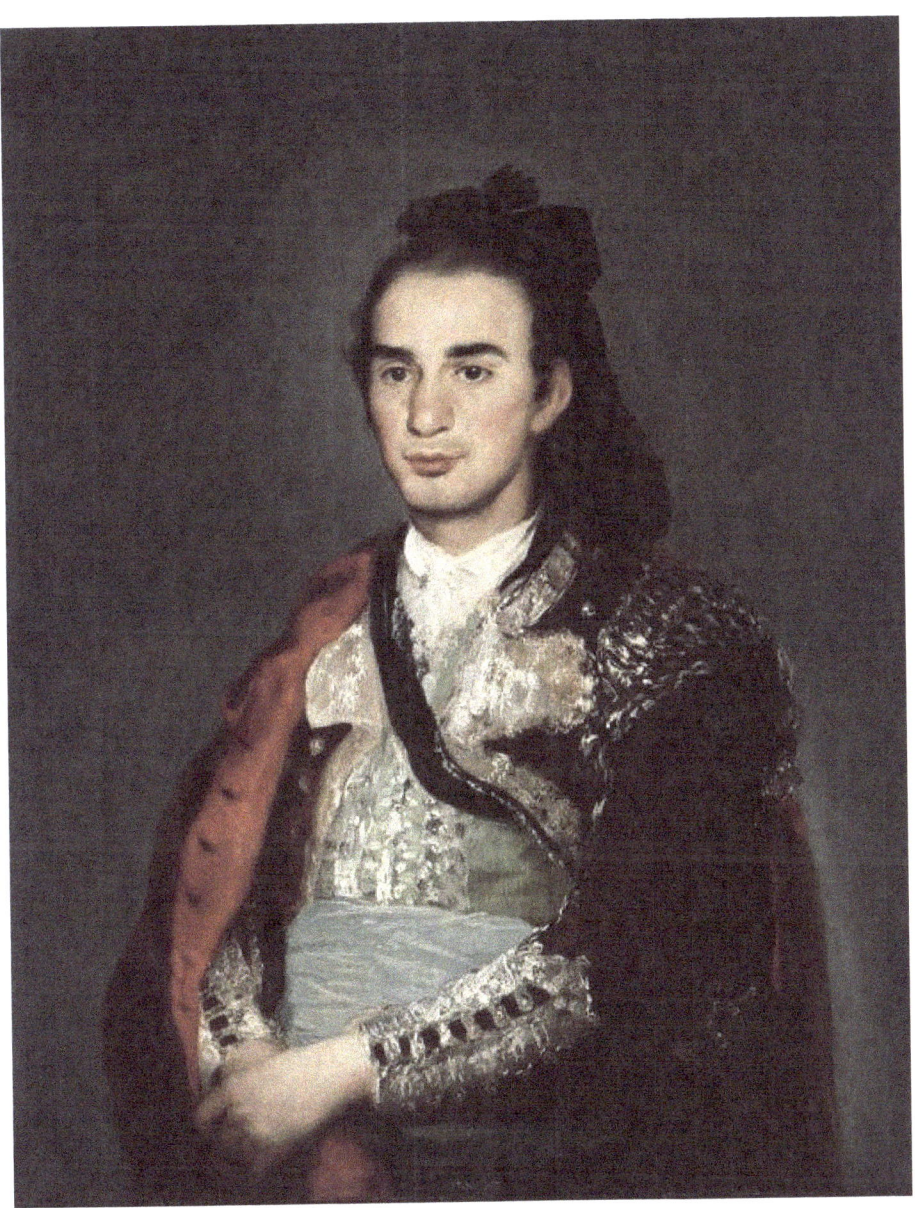

BULL FIGHTING

Children playing the bulls (1785)

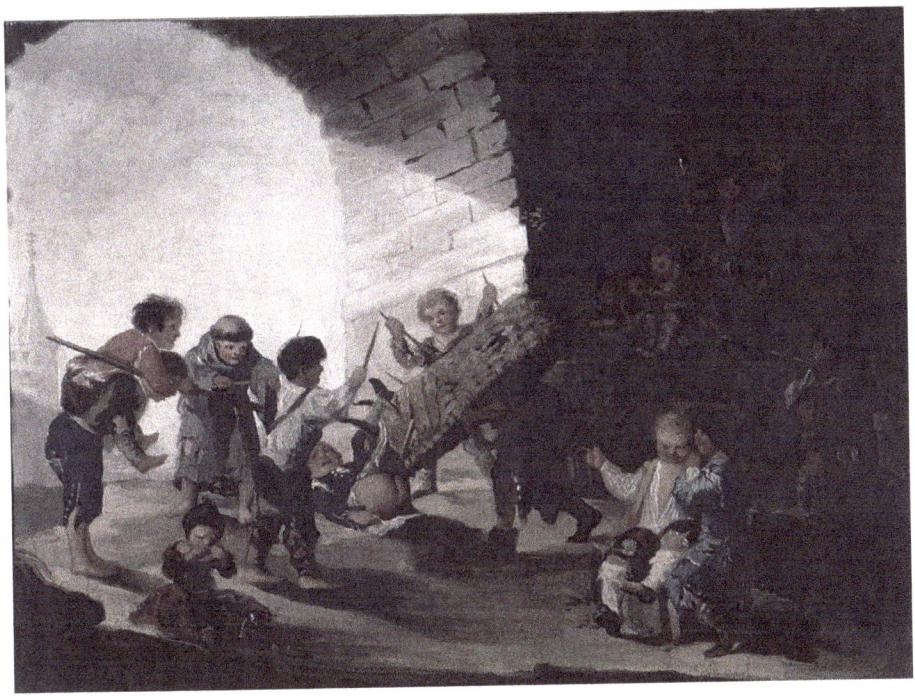

Bull section (1787)

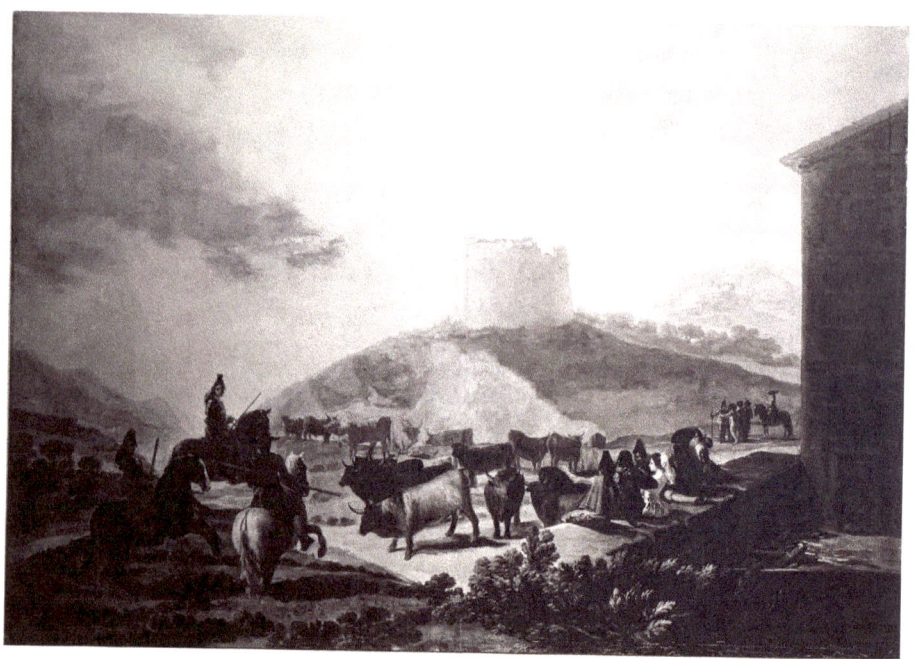

THE BULLS OF FRANCISCO DE GOYA

Clearing of the square   (1793)

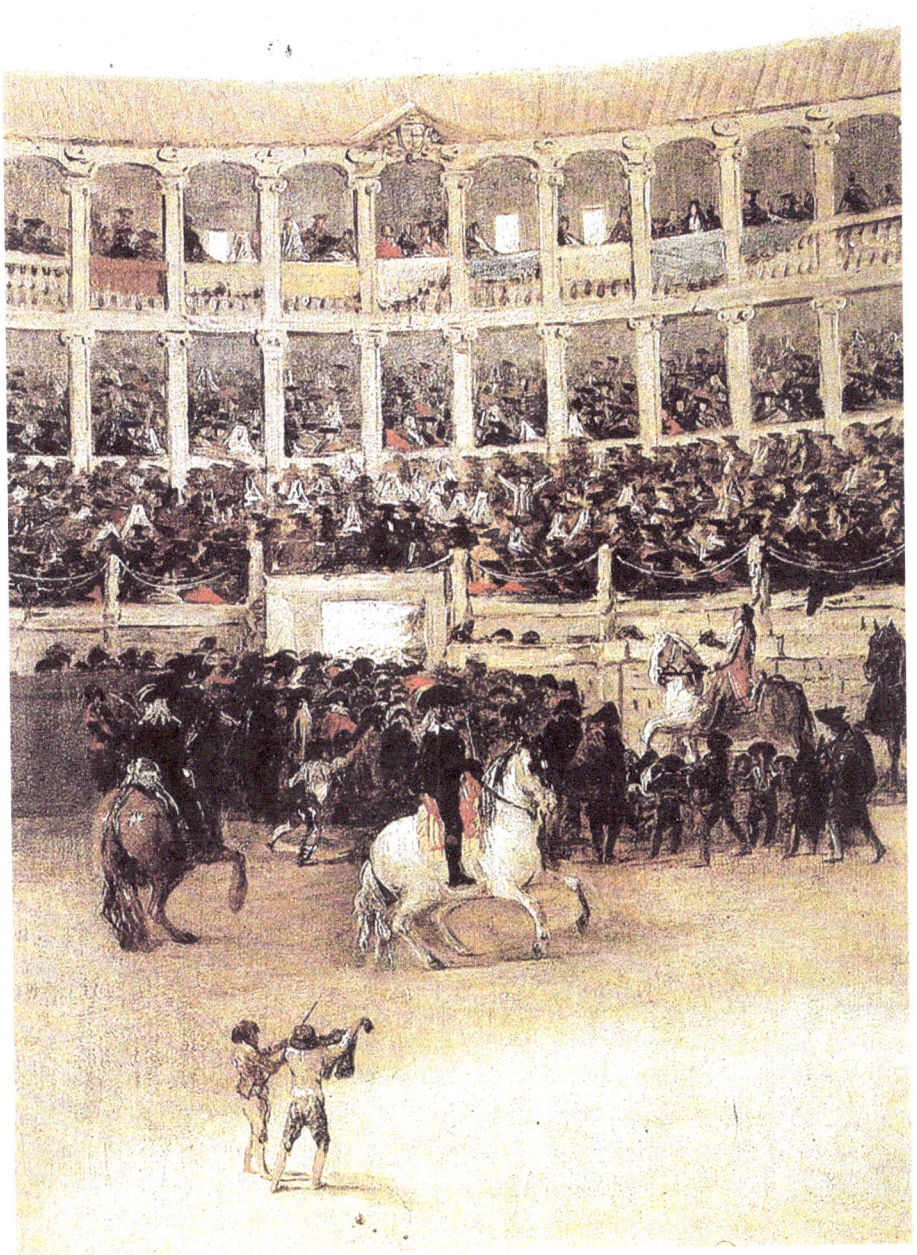

The Drag (1793)

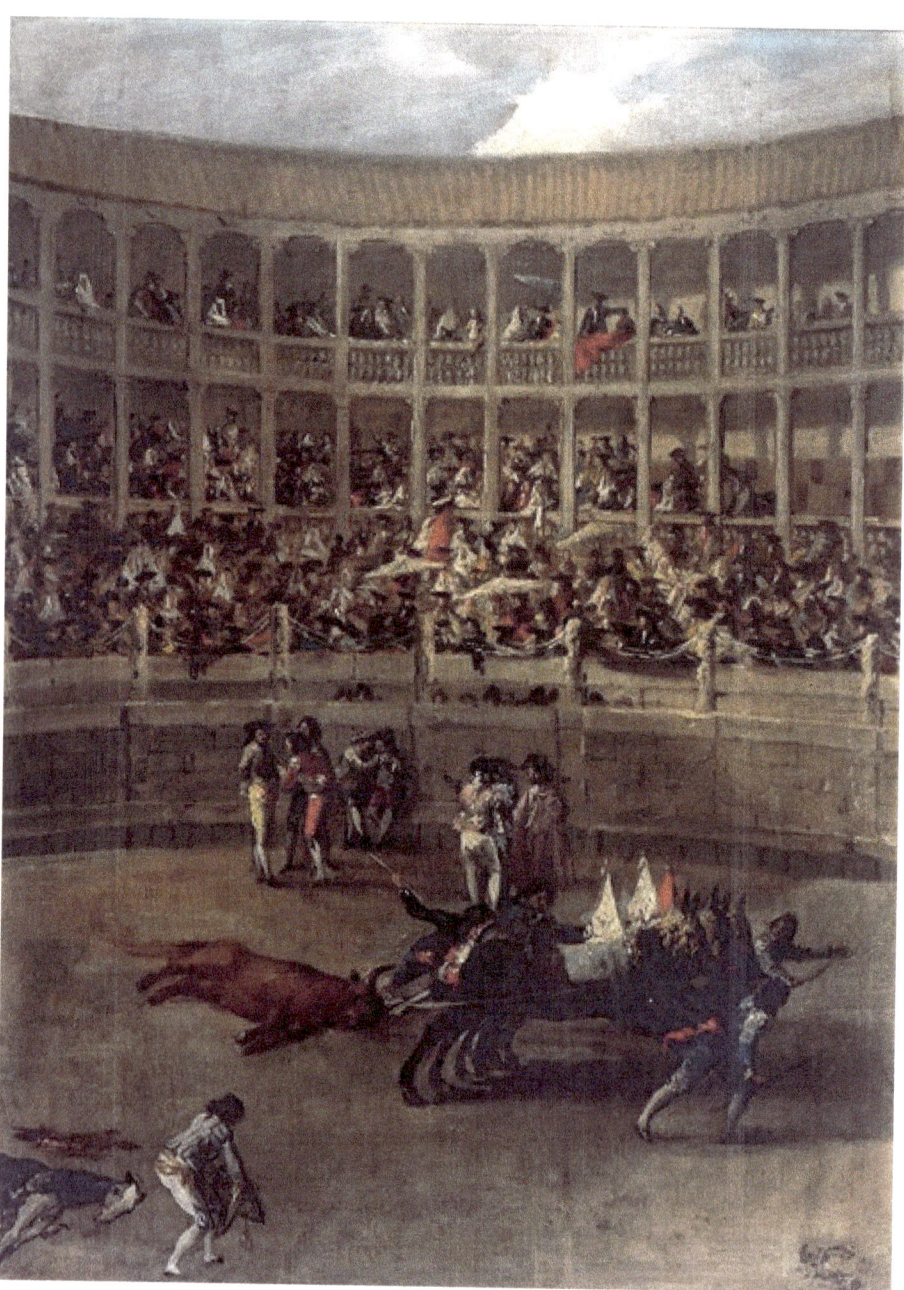

THE BULLS OF FRANCISCO DE GOYA

The enamored bull (1793)

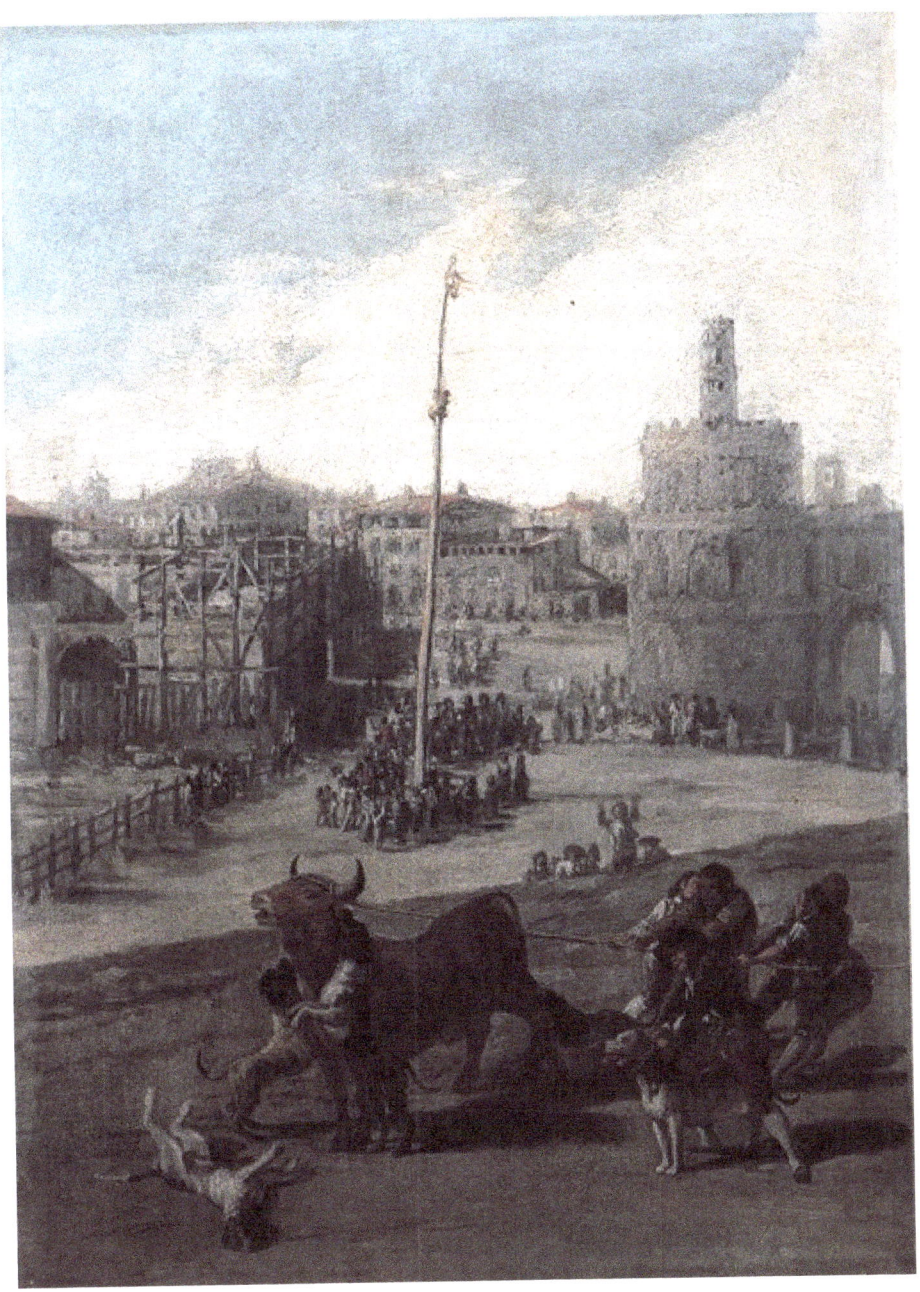

Picador caught by the bull (1793)

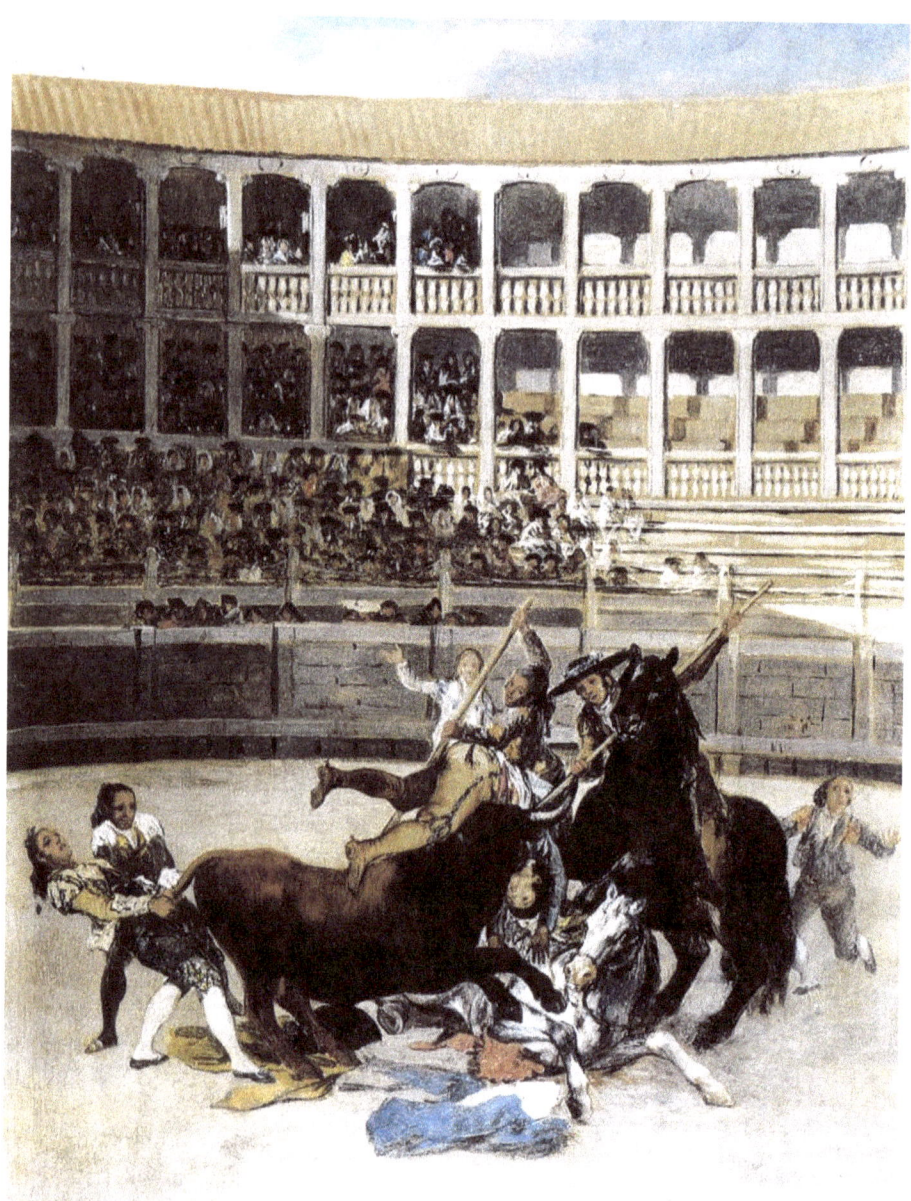

THE BULLS OF FRANCISCO DE GOYA

Luck of killing (1793)

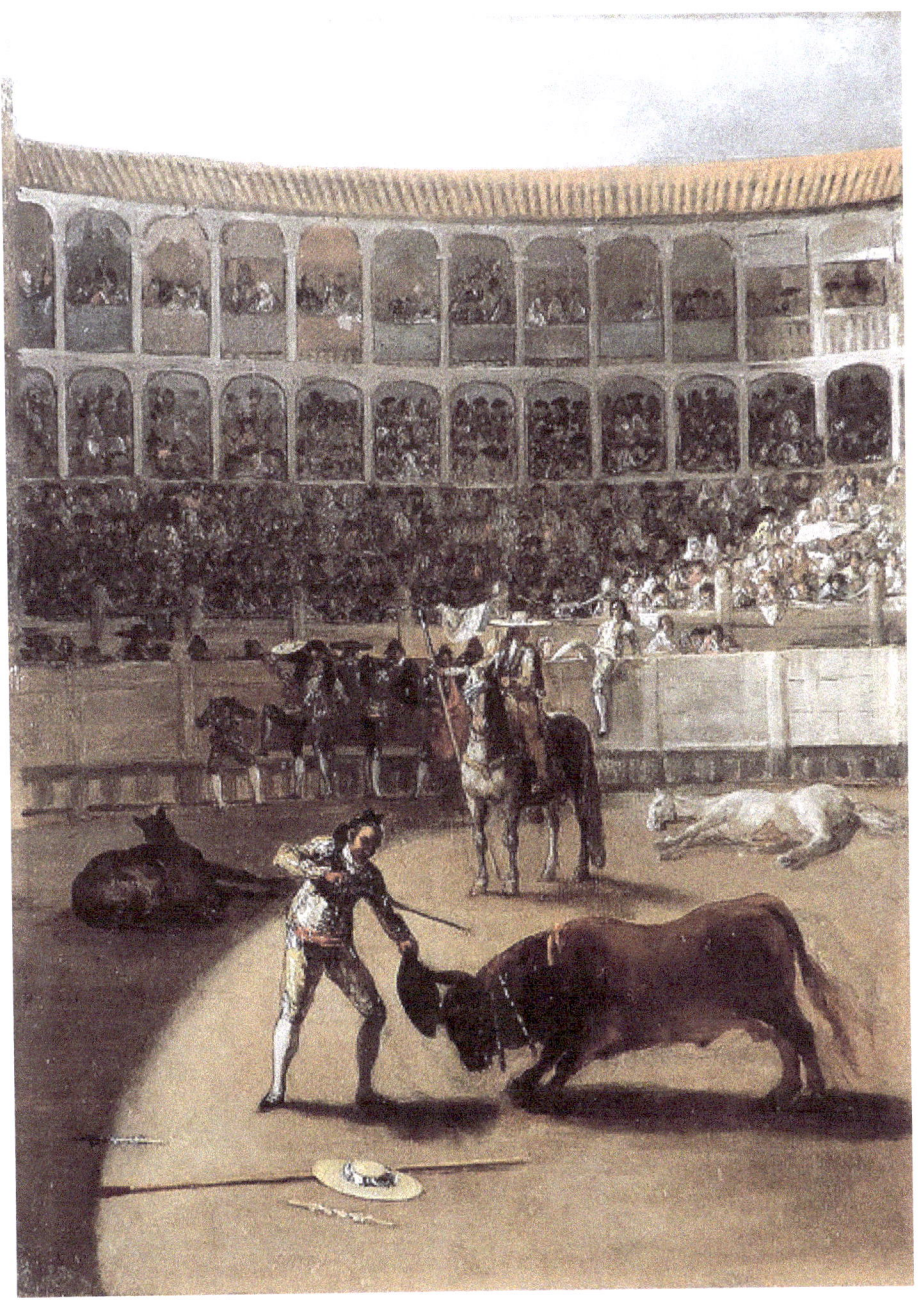

JOSÉ RENÉ CRUZ REVUELTAS

Bulls in the meadow (1794)

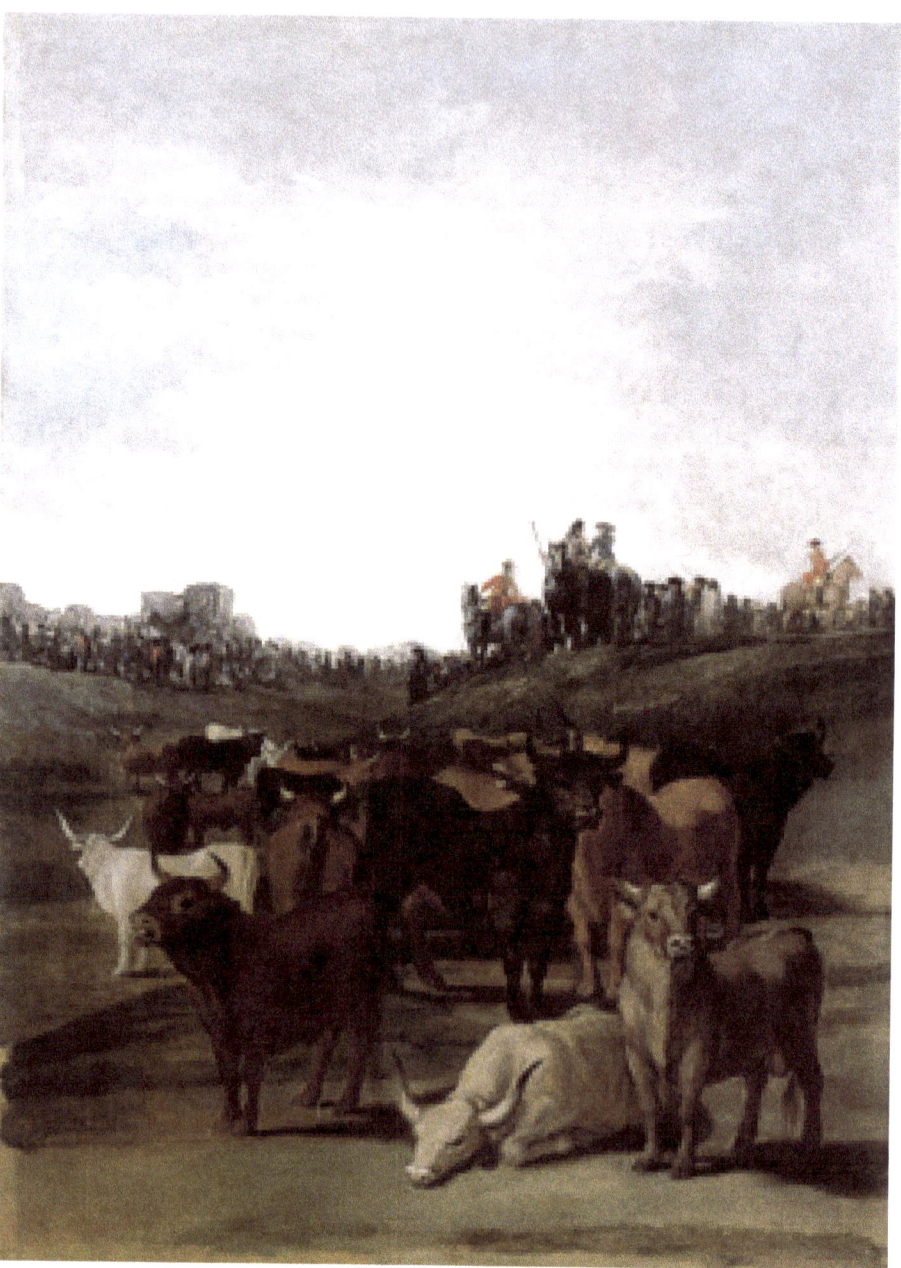

Banderillas in the field (1793)

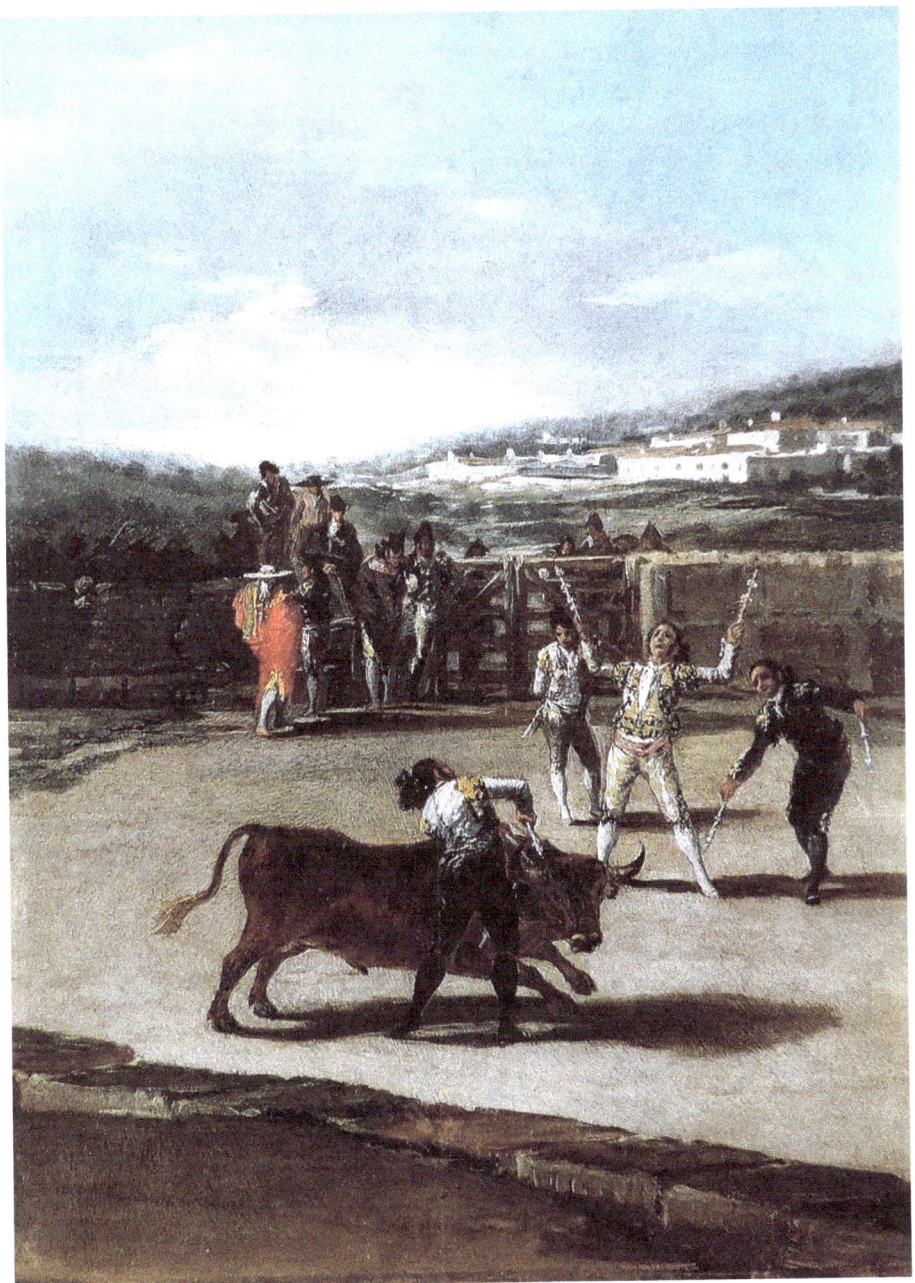

The death of the picador (1793)

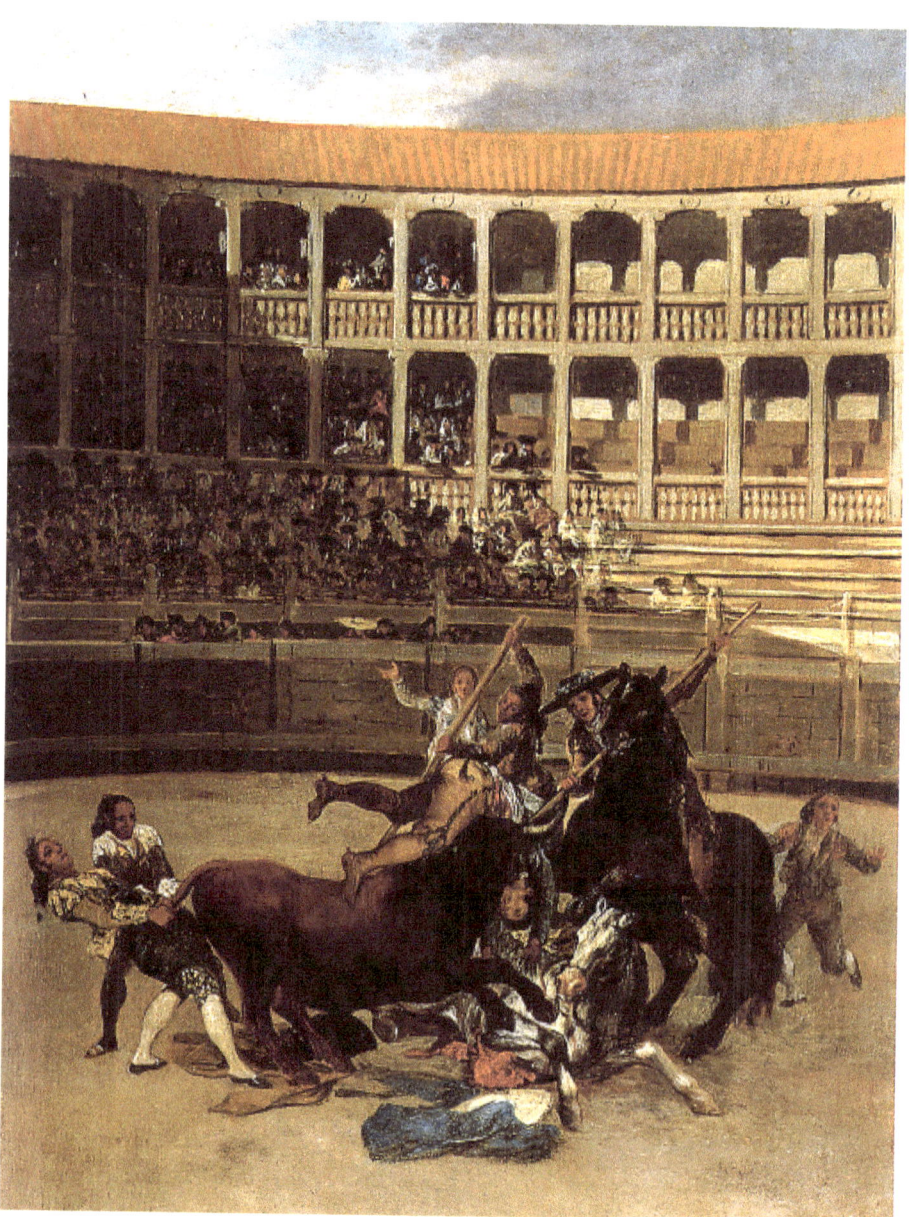

Bullfight in a town (1814)

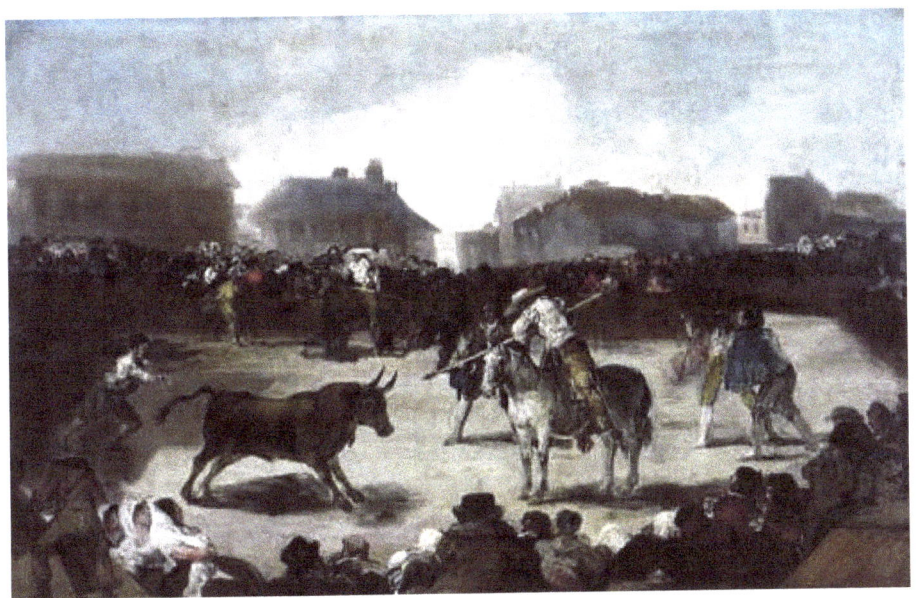

Bullfight in a divided square (1816)

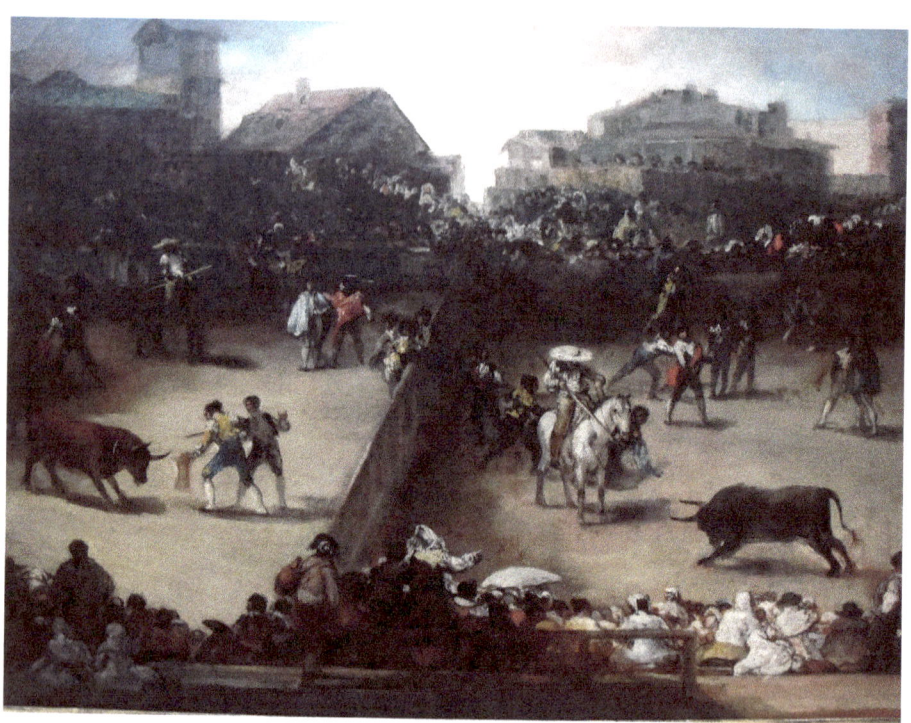

THE BULLS OF FRANCISCO DE GOYA

Luck of rods (1824)

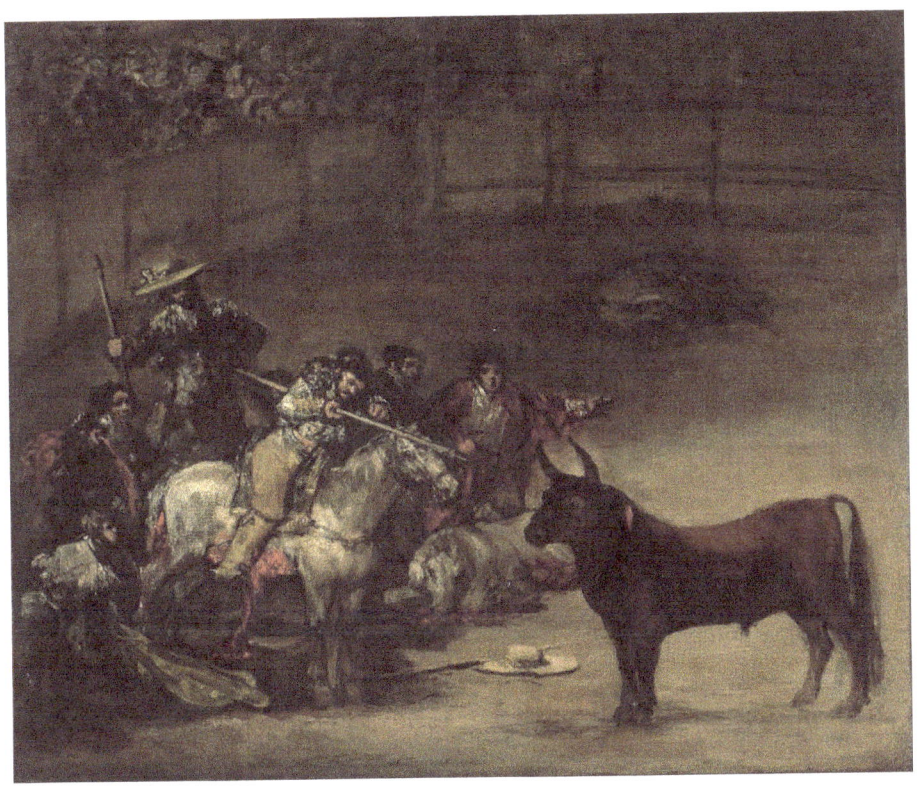

LA TAUROMAQUIA (1816)

Thirty-three engravings that Francisco de Goya published in 1816. These works were made slowly, without a specific plan.

Fall of a picador from his horse under the bull

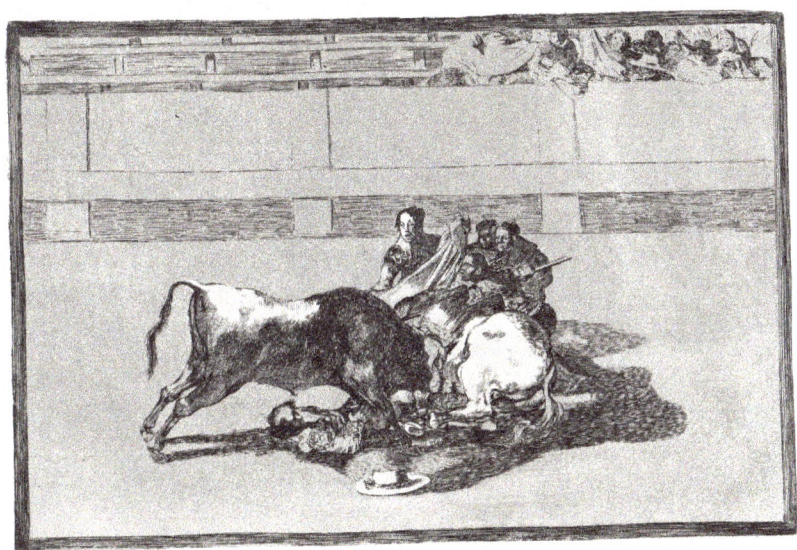

JOSÉ RENÉ CRUZ REVUELTAS

Banderillas of fire

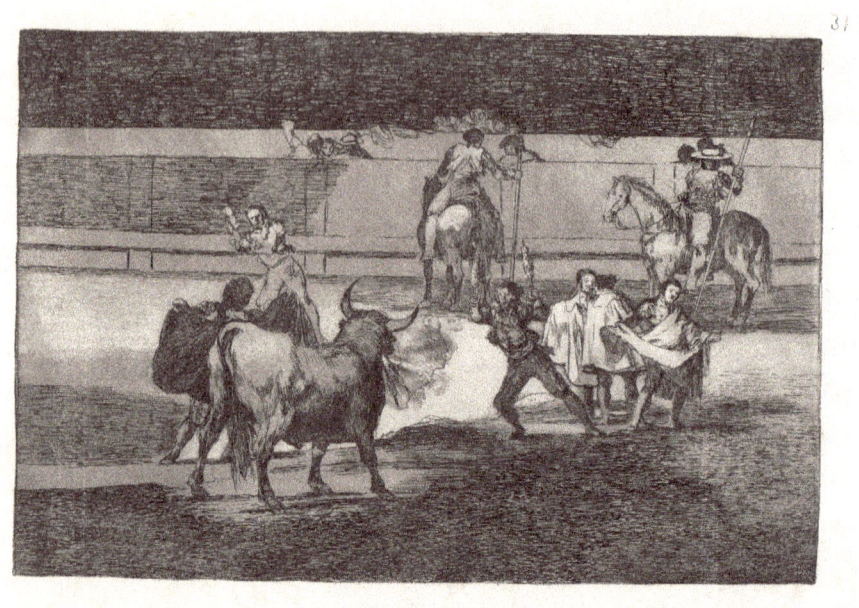

The unfortunate death of Pepe Illo in the square of Madrid

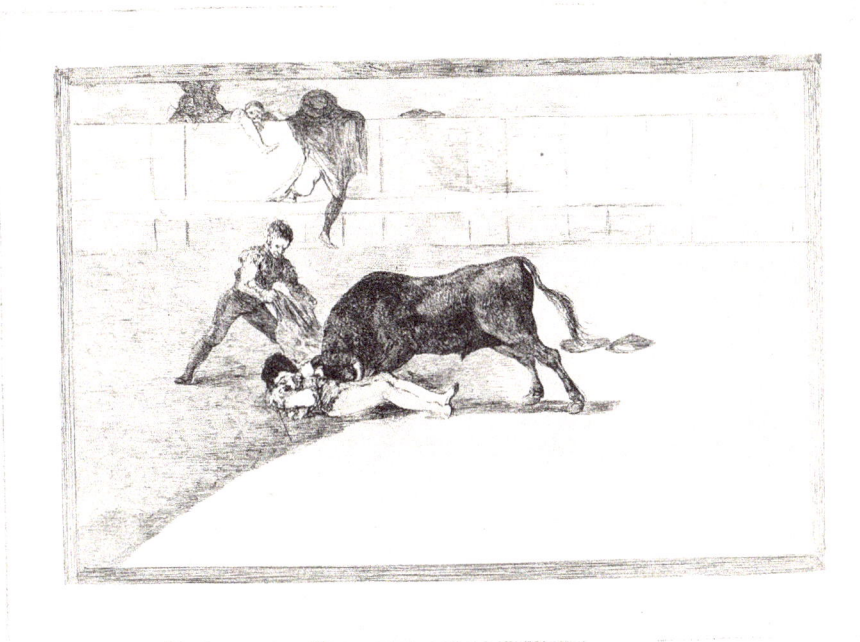

JOSÉ RENÉ CRUZ REVUELTAS

The bravery of Martincho in the plaza de Zaragoza

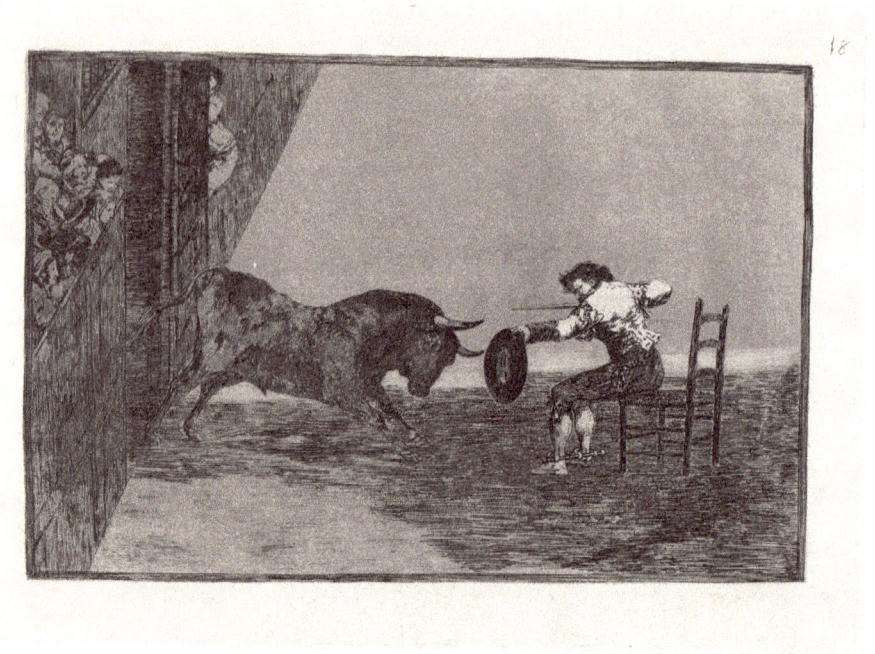

Capean another locked up

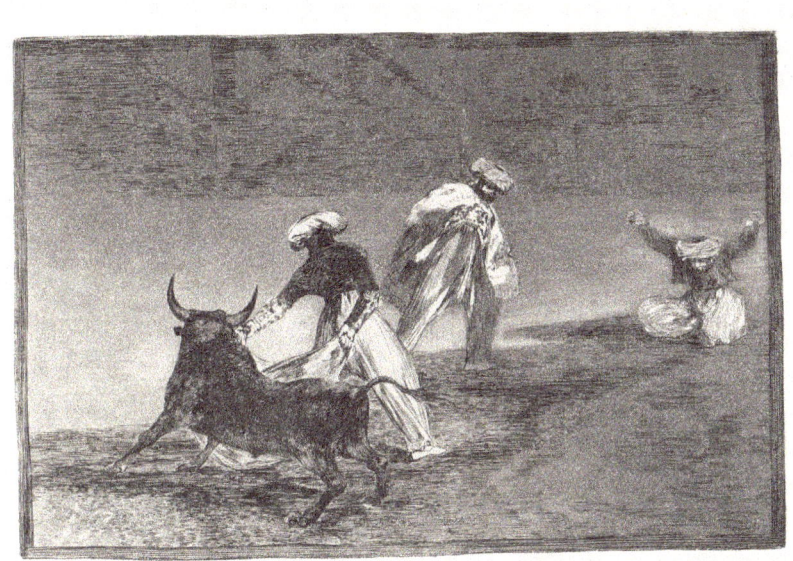

Carlos V. spearing a bull in the plaza of Valladolid

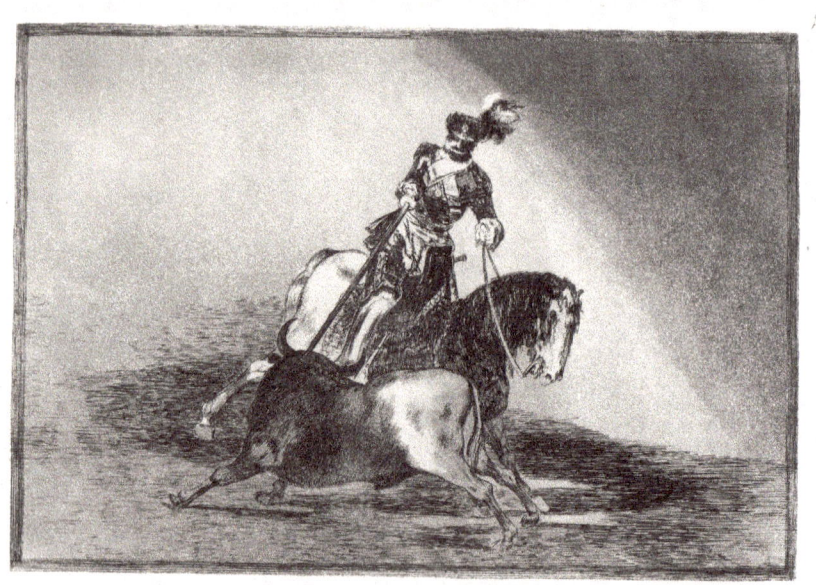

THE BULLS OF FRANCISCO DE GOYA

Goring the moor in the bullring

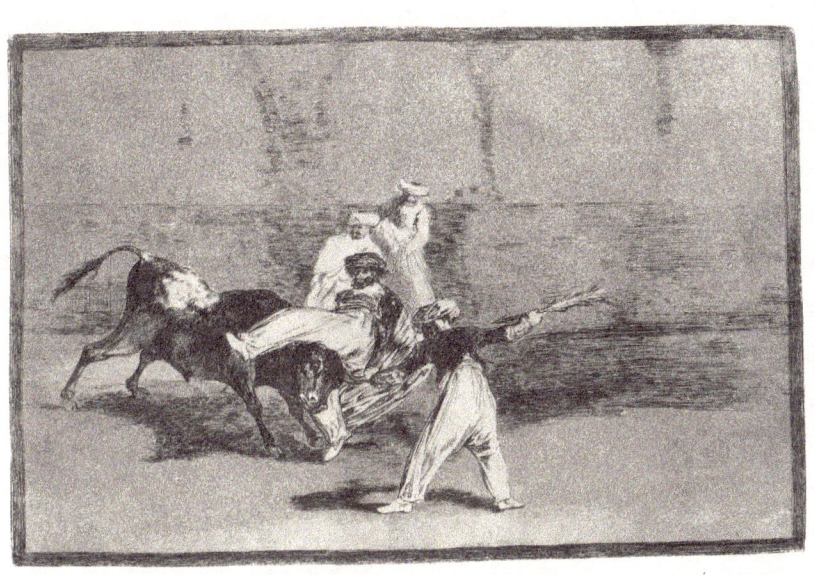

Misfortunes that occurred in the laying of the Madrid bullring, and death of the mayor of Torrejón

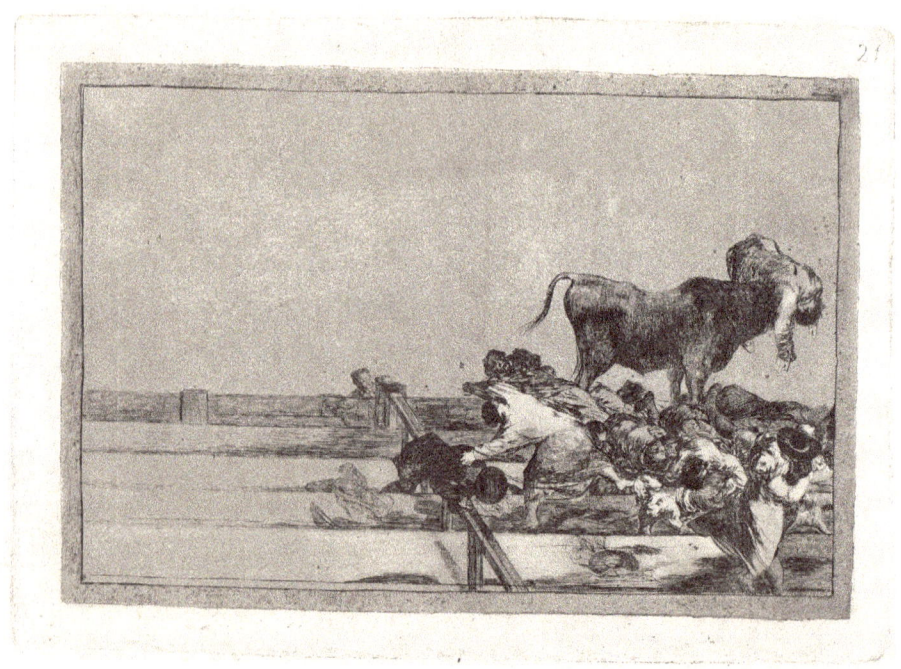

Hambling of the populace with crescent spears, banderillas and other weapons

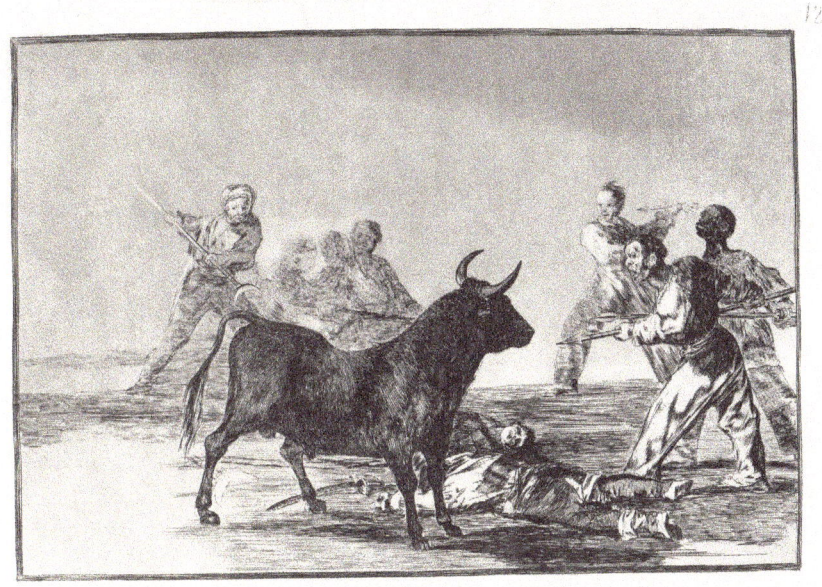

JOSÉ RENÉ CRUZ REVUELTAS

Two groups of picadores run over by a single bull

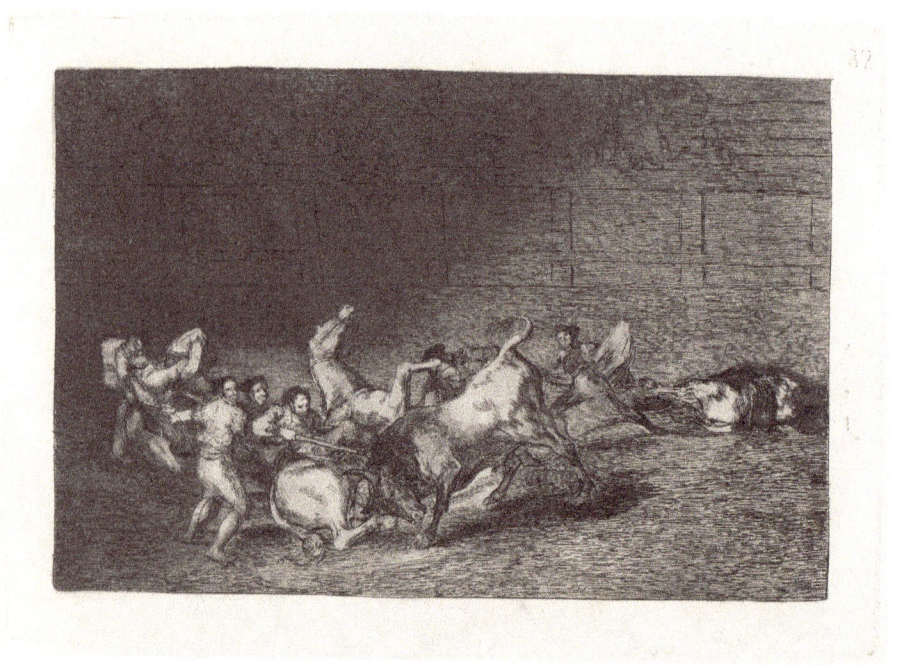

They throw dogs to the bullring

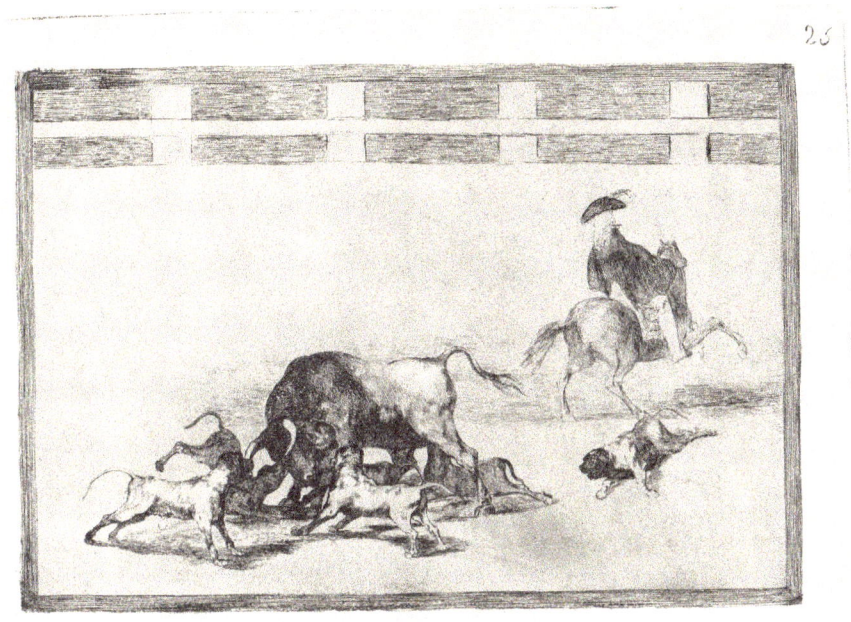

JOSÉ RENÉ CRUZ REVUELTAS

The spirited blue moor is the first to lance bulls in order

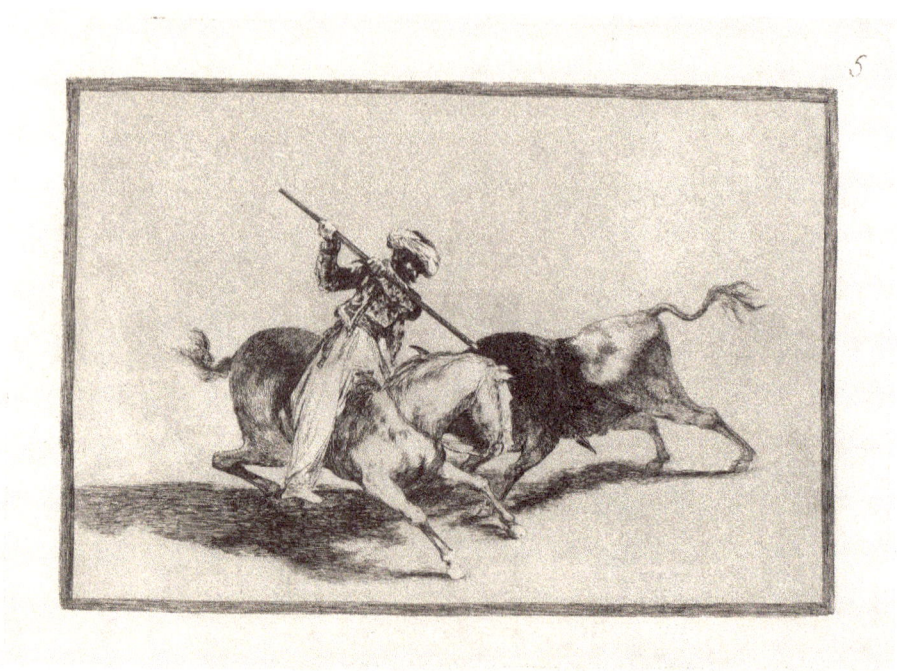

*The famous varilarguero
Fernando del Toro, forcing
the beast with his pole*

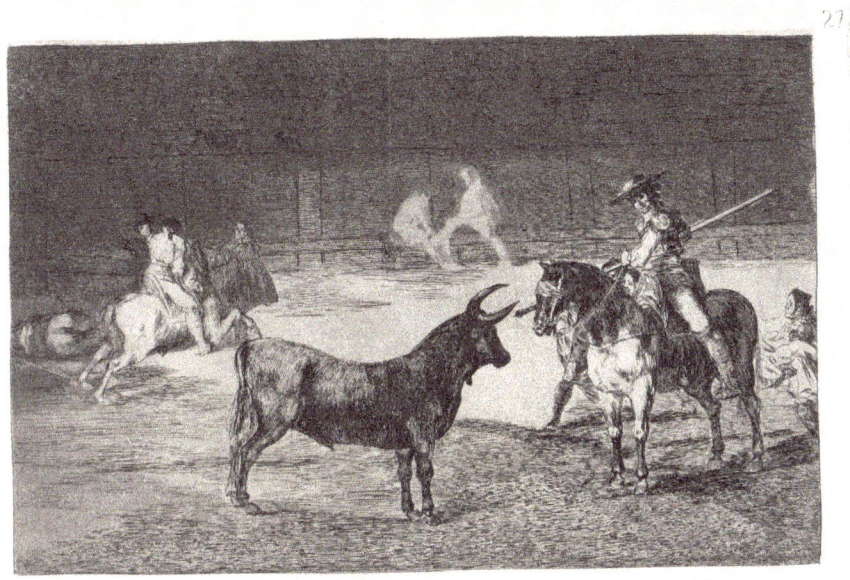

El Cid Campeador spearing another bull (1816)

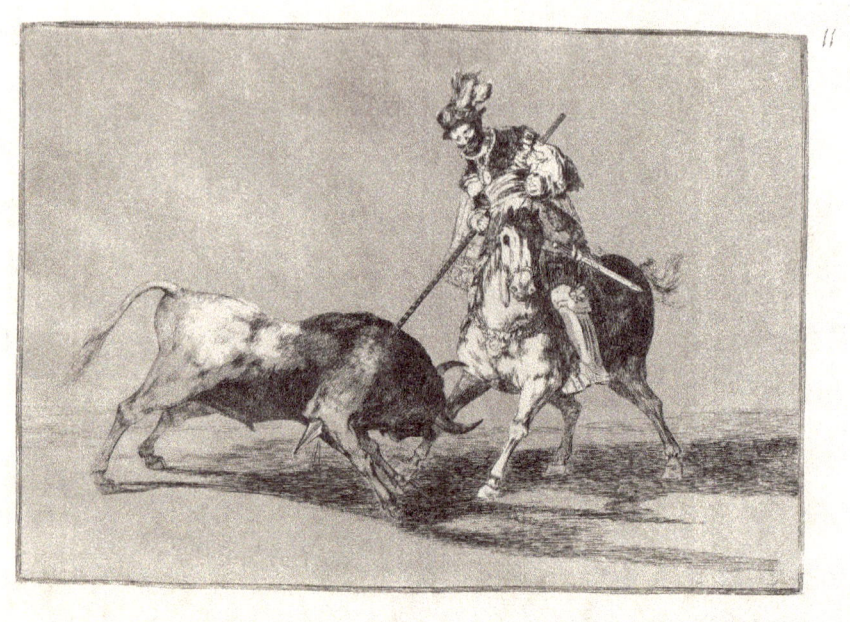

The clever student of Falces, cloaked, mocks the bull with his antics

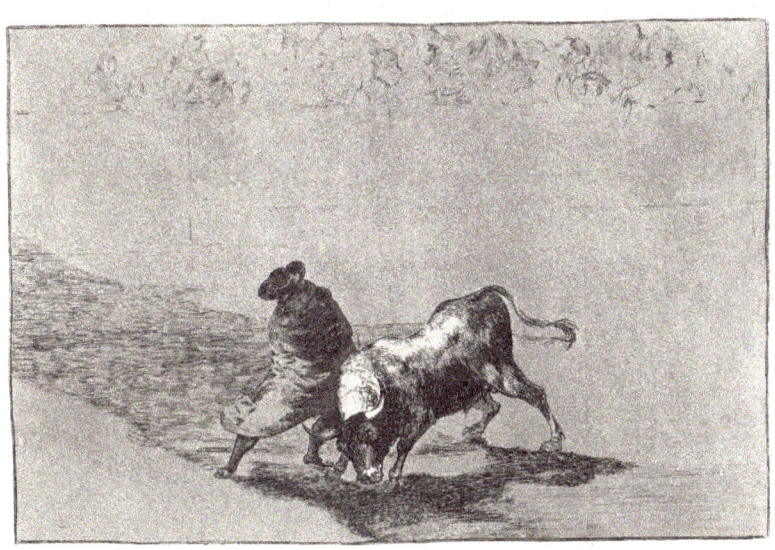

JOSÉ RENÉ CRUZ REVUELTAS

The brave Rendón biting a bull, whose destiny was to die in the bull field of Madrid

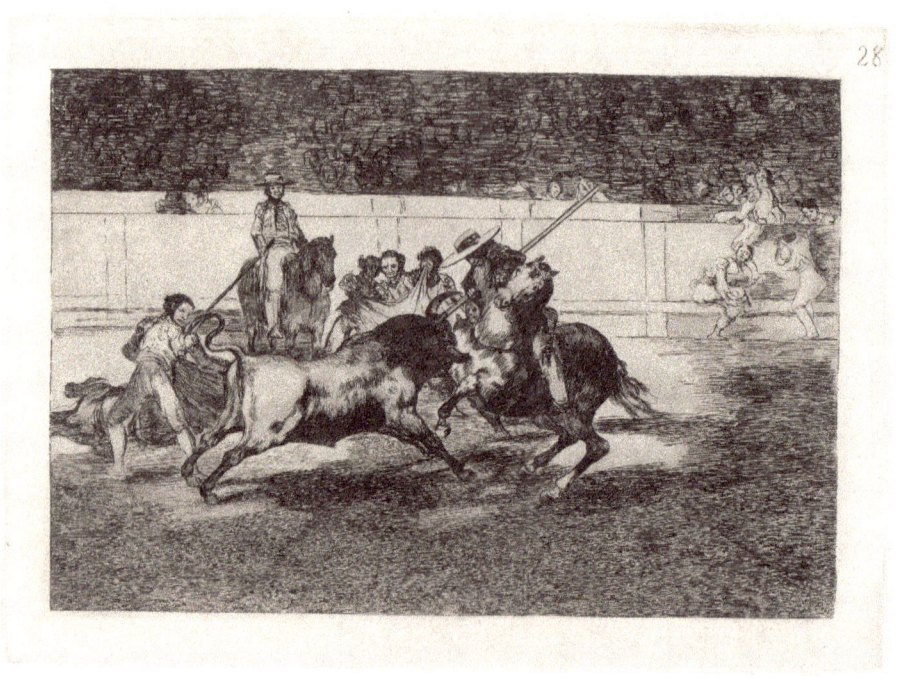

The famous Martincho putting banderillas to the quiebro

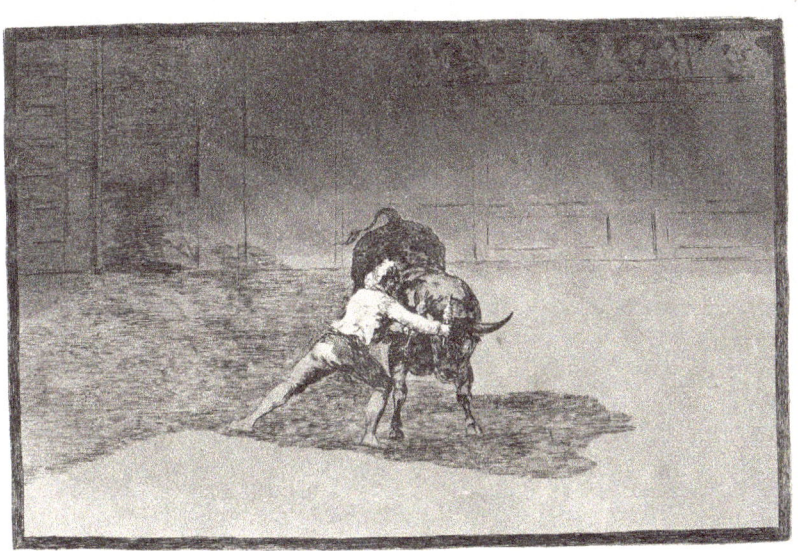

Ceballos himself mounted on another bull breaks spears in the bull field of Madrid

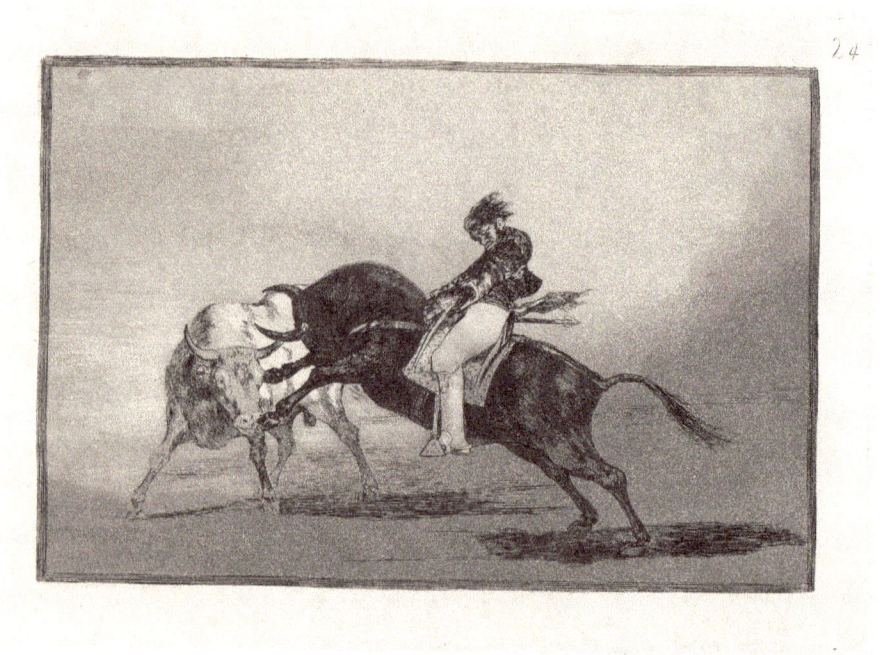

THE BULLS OF FRANCISCO DE GOYA

He himself overturns a bull in the bull field of Madrid

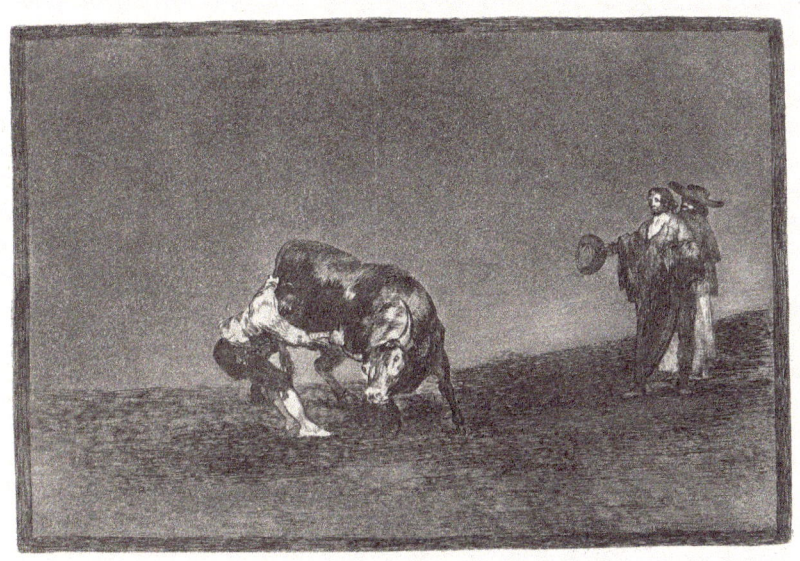

JOSÉ RENÉ CRUZ REVUELTAS

The unfortunate death of Pepe Illo in the plaza of Madrid

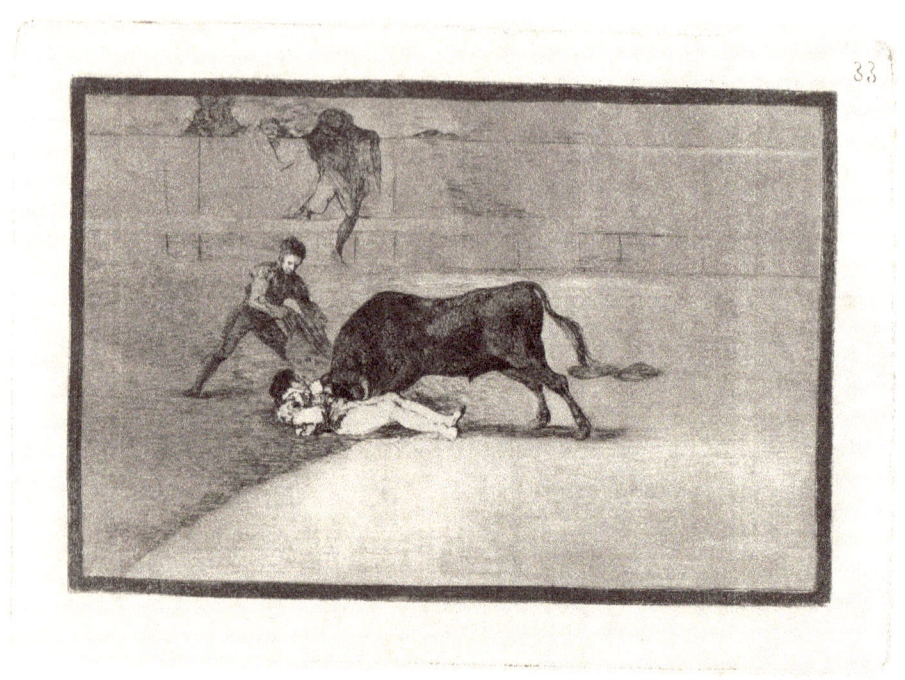

Lightness and audacity of Juanito Apinani in Madrid

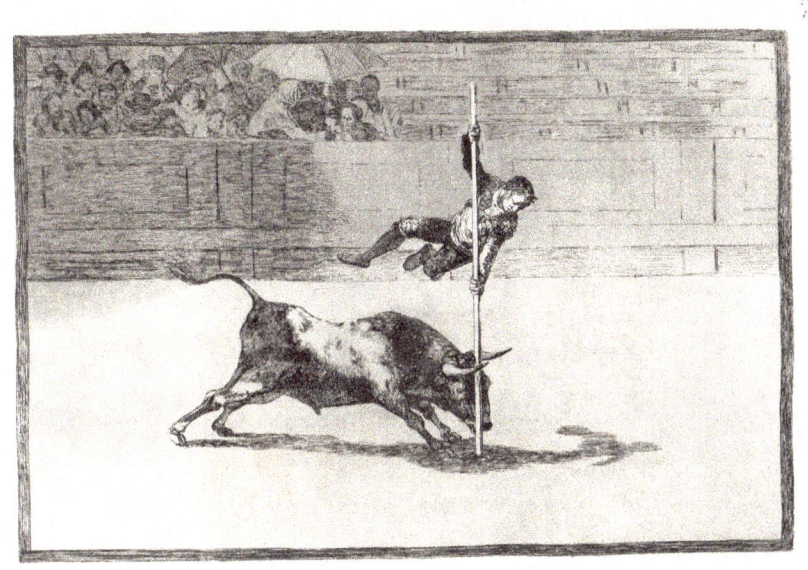

JOSÉ RENÉ CRUZ REVUELTAS

The moors lance a bull in the field

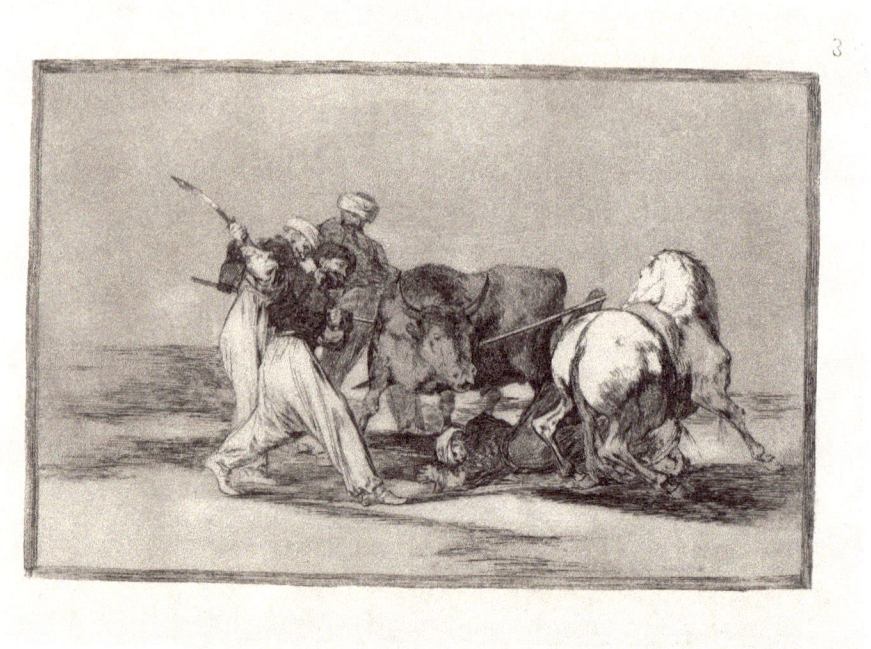

The moors make another capeo in the square with their bathrobe

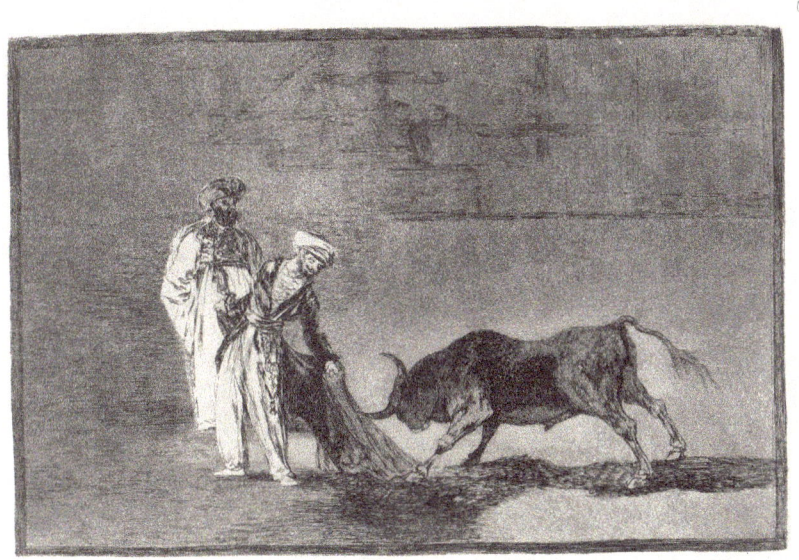

JOSÉ RENÉ CRUZ REVUELTAS

Mariano Ceballos, alias the Indian, kills the bull from his horse

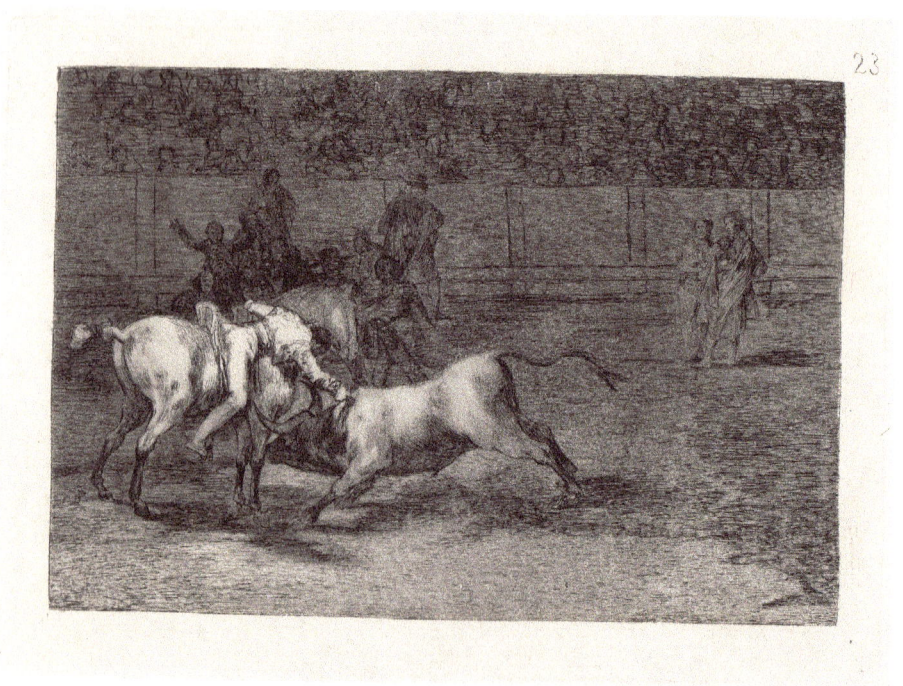

Way in which the ancient spaniards hunted bulls on horseback in the countryside

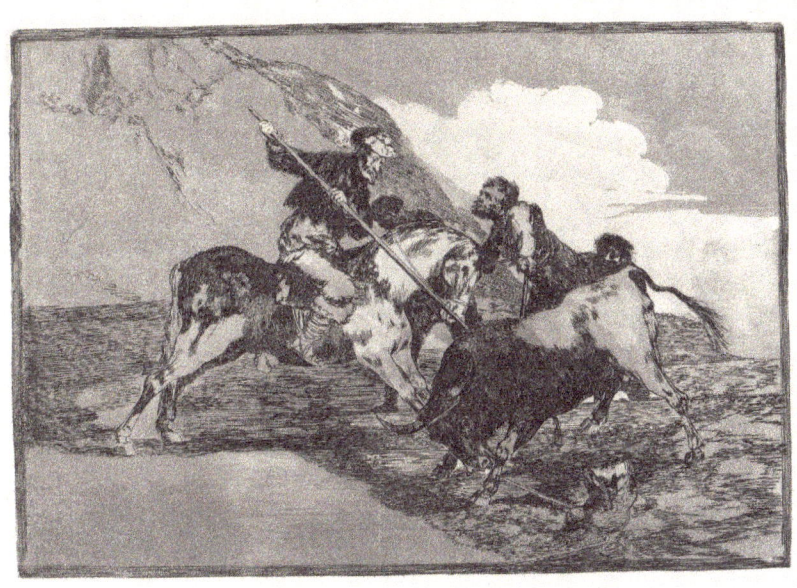

Origin of laying banderillas

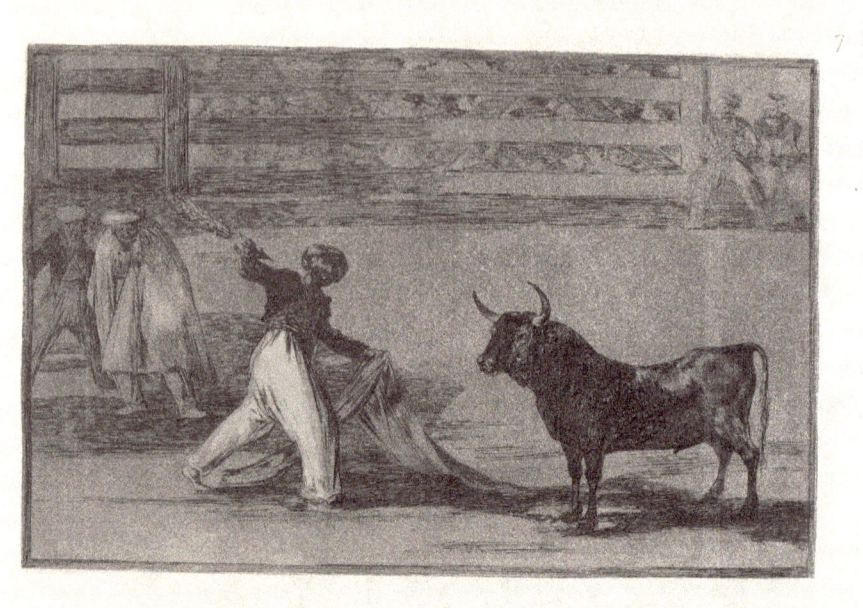

THE BULLS OF FRANCISCO DE GOYA

Another madness in the same square

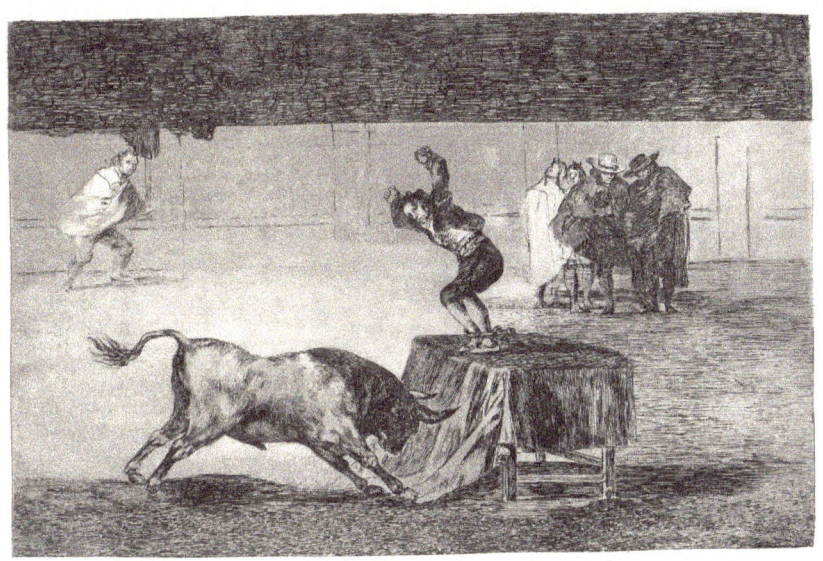

JOSÉ RENÉ CRUZ REVUELTAS

Another way of hunting on foot

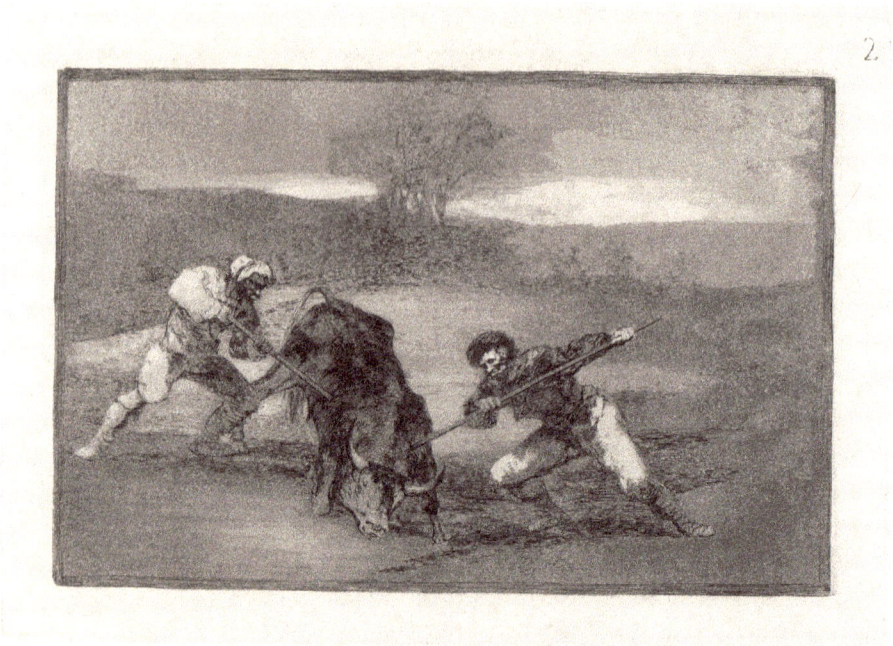

The moors use donkeys as a barrier to defend themselves against the bull whose horns have been tipped with balls

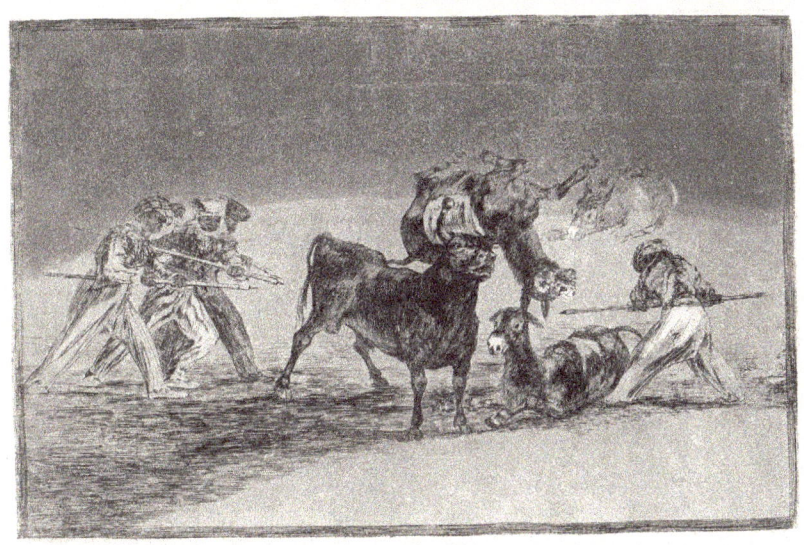

Pedro Romero killing a standing bull

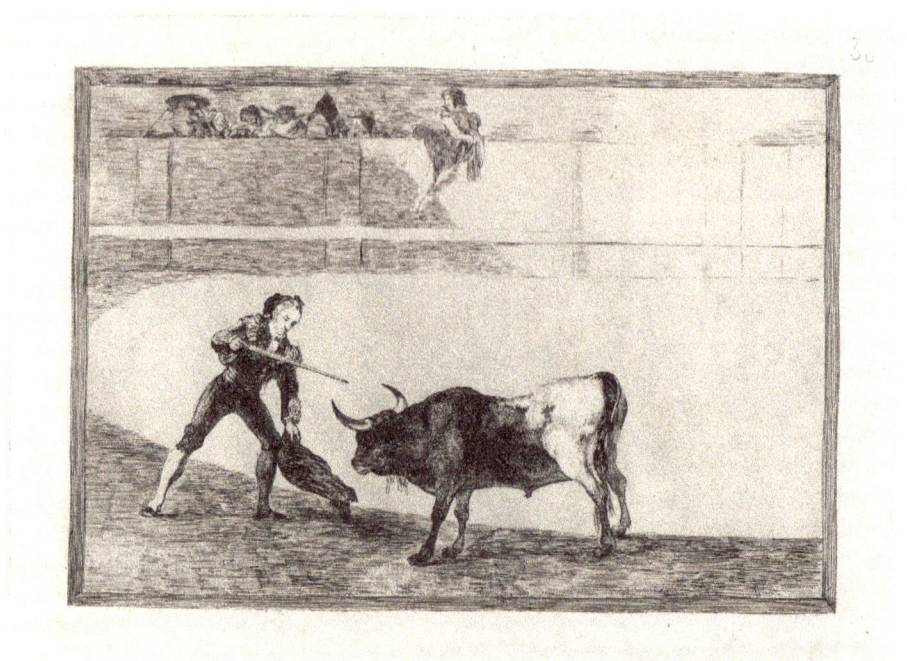

THE BULLS OF FRANCISCO DE GOYA

Pepe Illo making the cut to the bull 'Recorte'

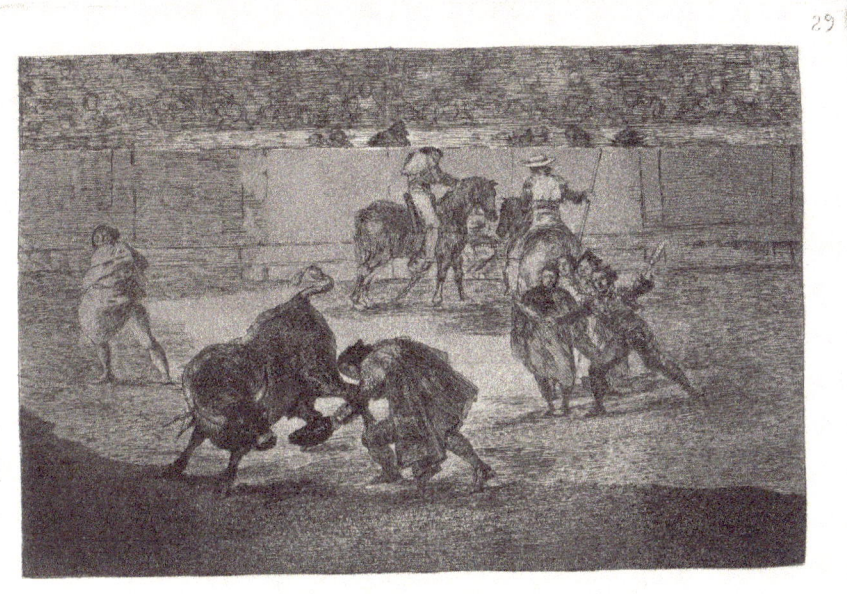

A spanish gentleman in the square breaking rejoncillos without the help of the pimps

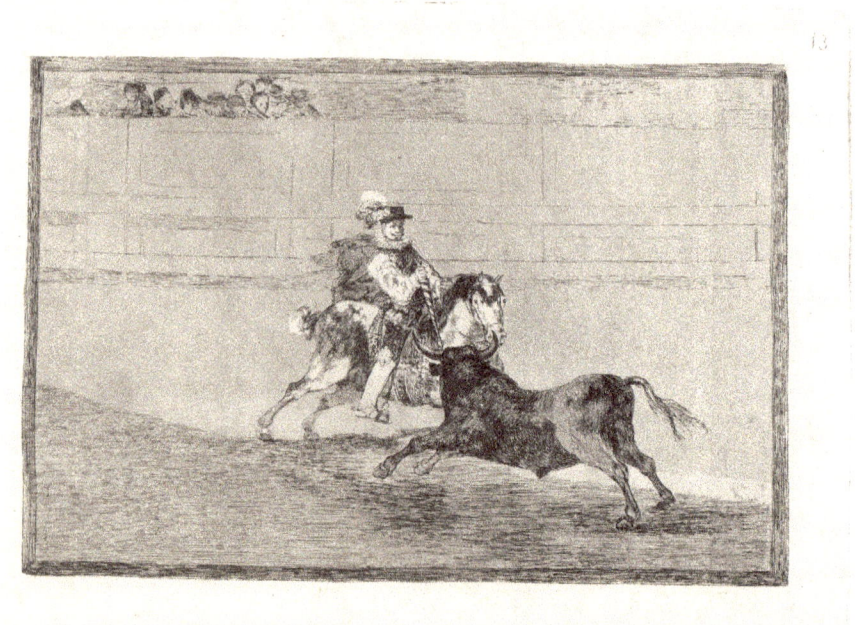

THE BULLS OF FRANCISCO DE GOYA

A spanish knight kills a bull after losing his horse

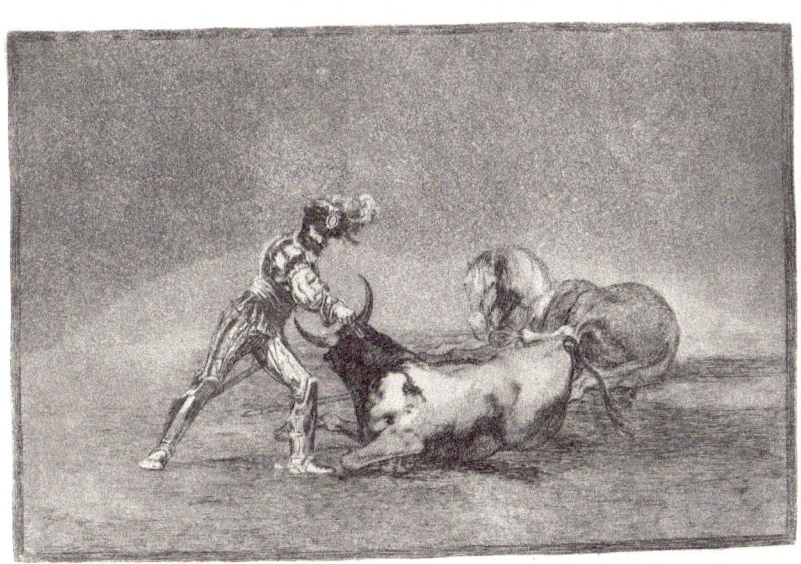

JOSÉ RENÉ CRUZ REVUELTAS

Manly courage of the famous Pajuelera in Zaragoza

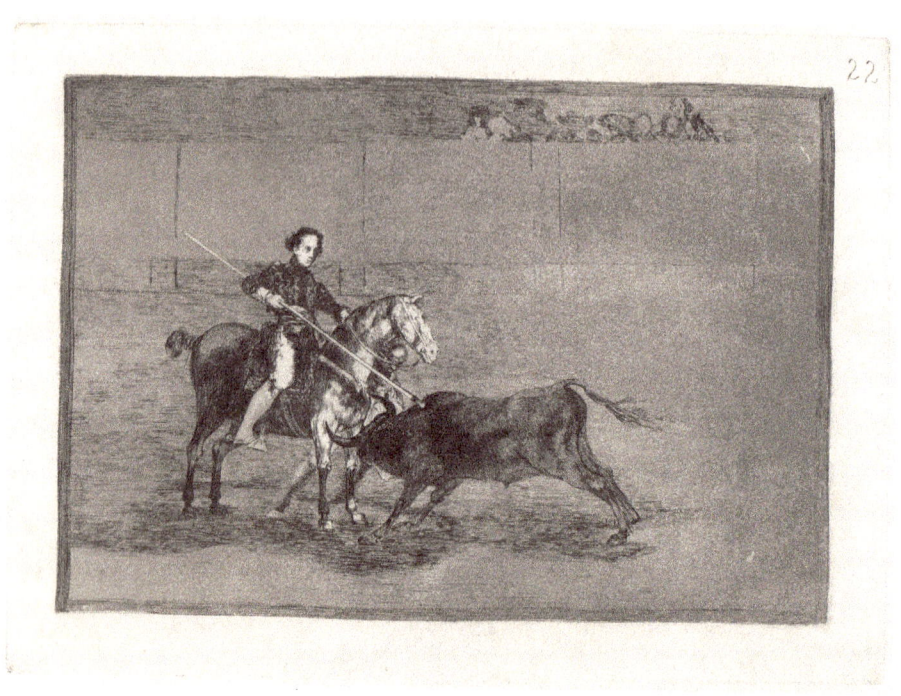

A gentleman in the square breaking a rejoncillo with the help of a pimp

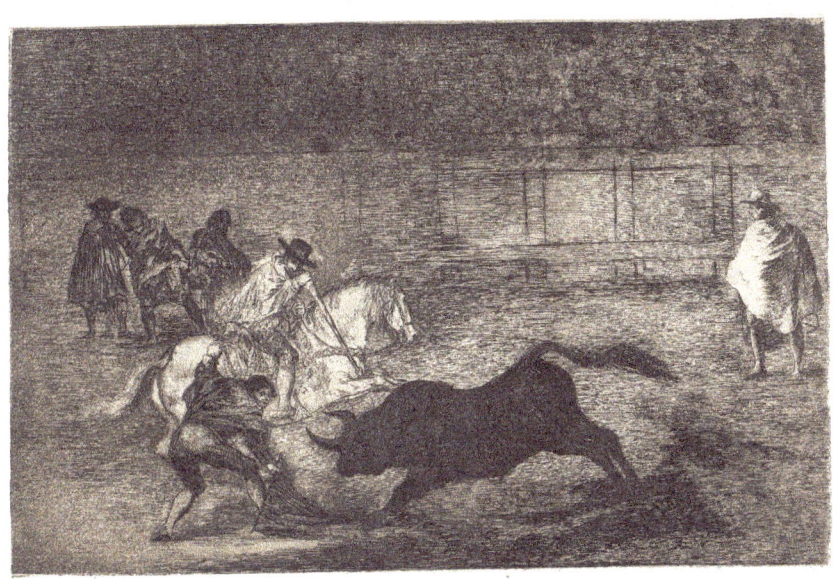

JOSÉ RENÉ CRUZ REVUELTAS

Unfortunate charge of a powerful bull

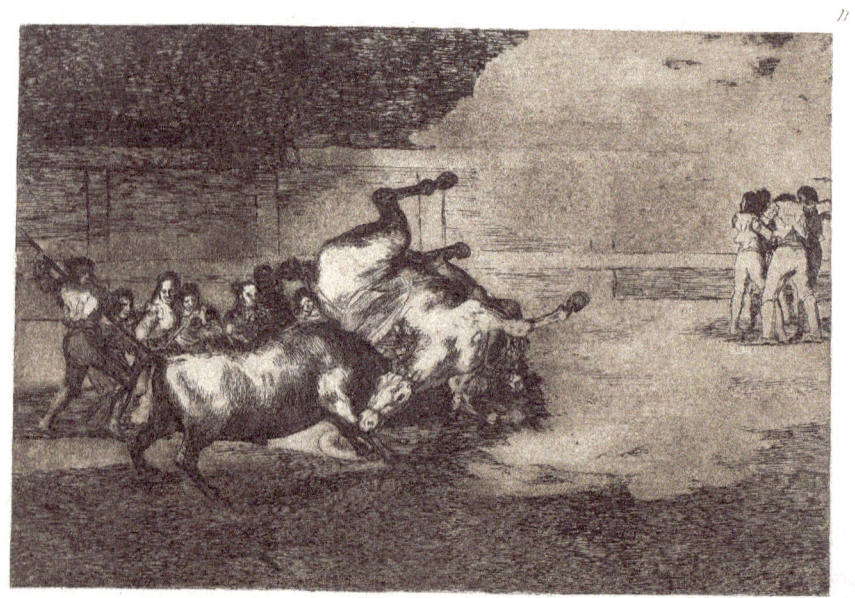

Dogs to the bull

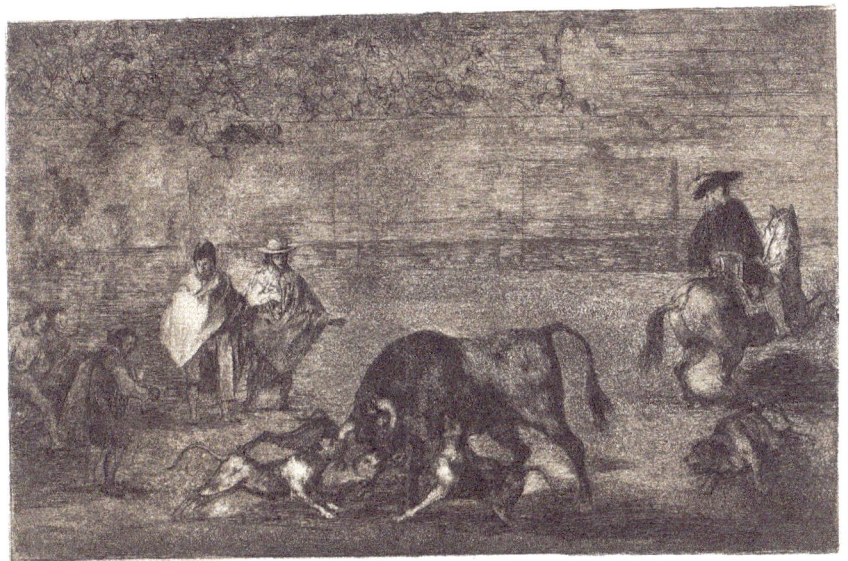

A varilarguero, mounted on the shoulders of a pimp, bites the bull

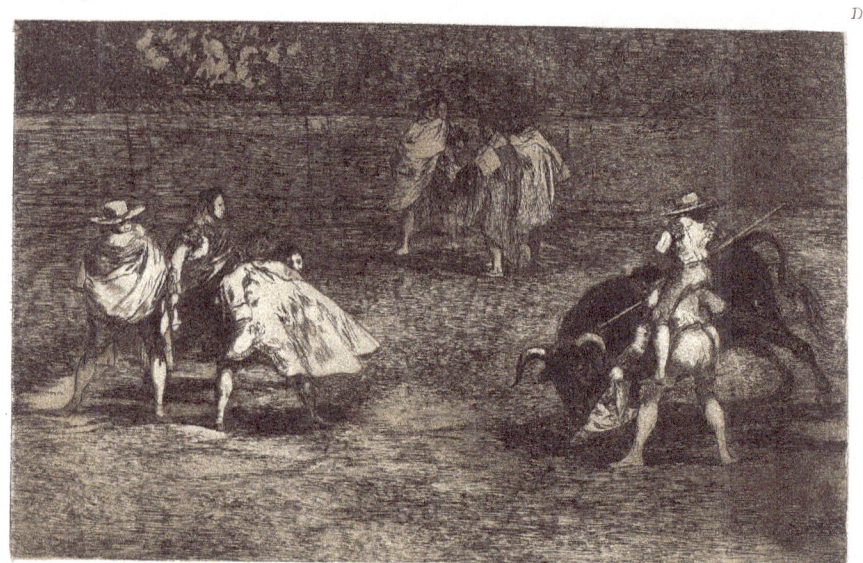

Fright and confusion in the defense of a caught pimp

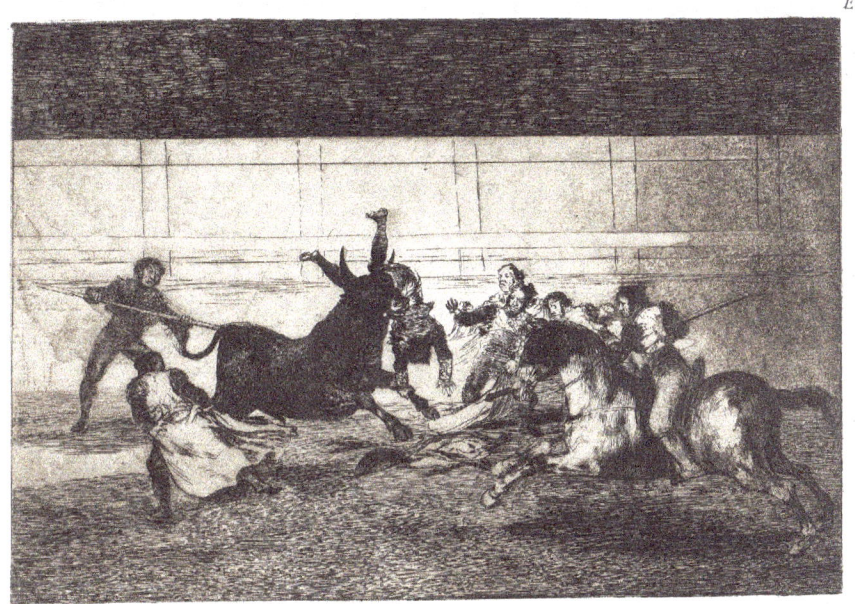

JOSÉ RENÉ CRUZ REVUELTAS

Varilarguero and pimps removing a caught bullfighter

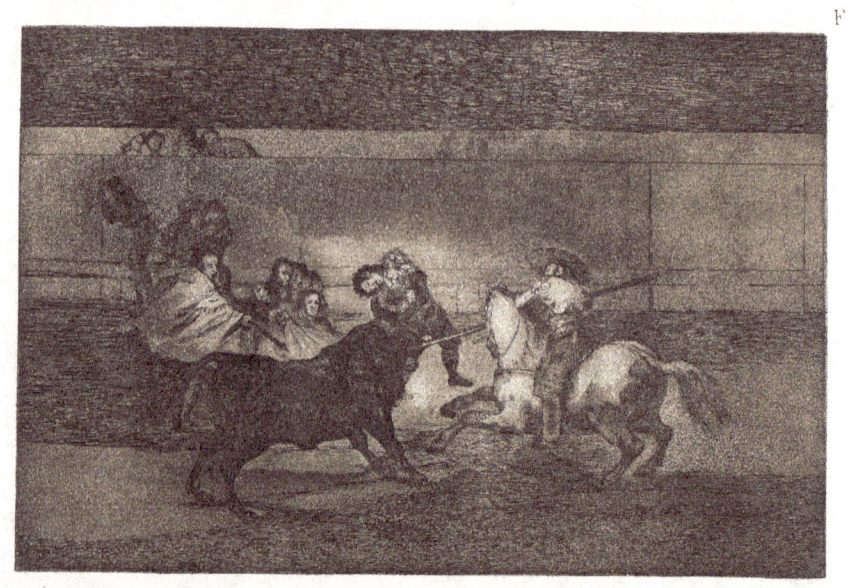

Mojiganga show

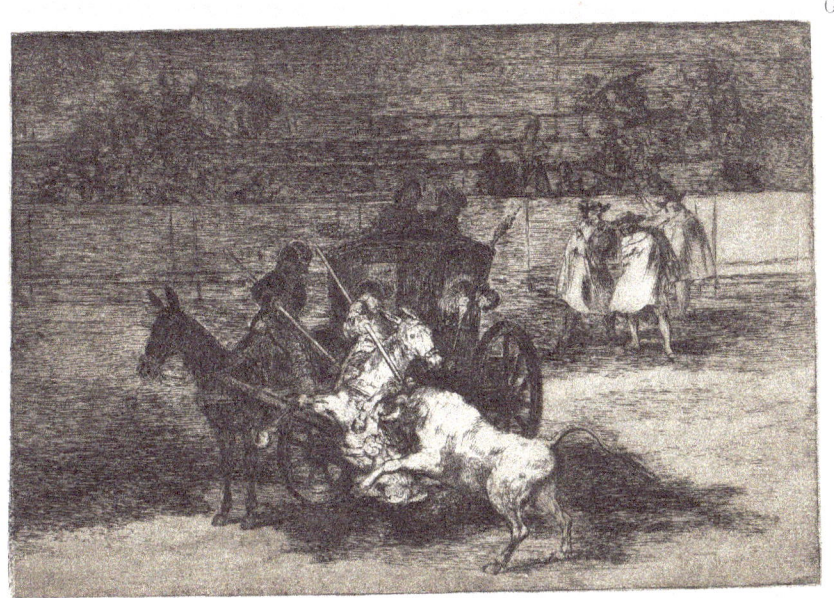

BORDEAUX

The lithographs of the Bordeaux bulls were made during 1824 and 1825 in the French city of Bordeaux. Unlike La tauromaquia, these works reflect professional bullfights and the sets of well-known bullfighters, together with the bullfighters, the collective brutalization of the masses is also reflected.

Angry bull

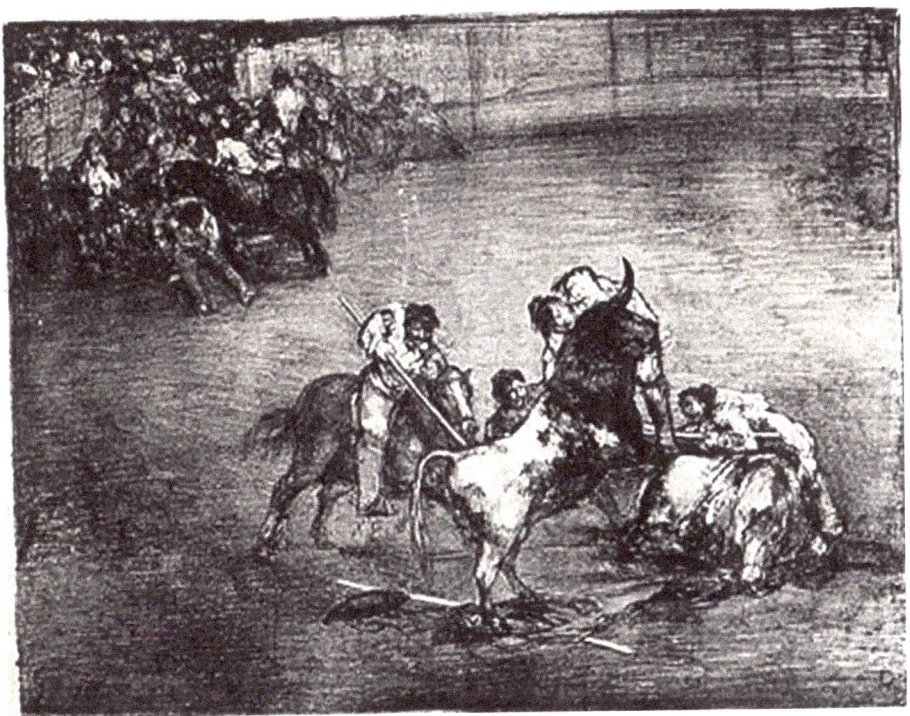

JOSÉ RENÉ CRUZ REVUELTAS

The famous American, Mariano Ceballos

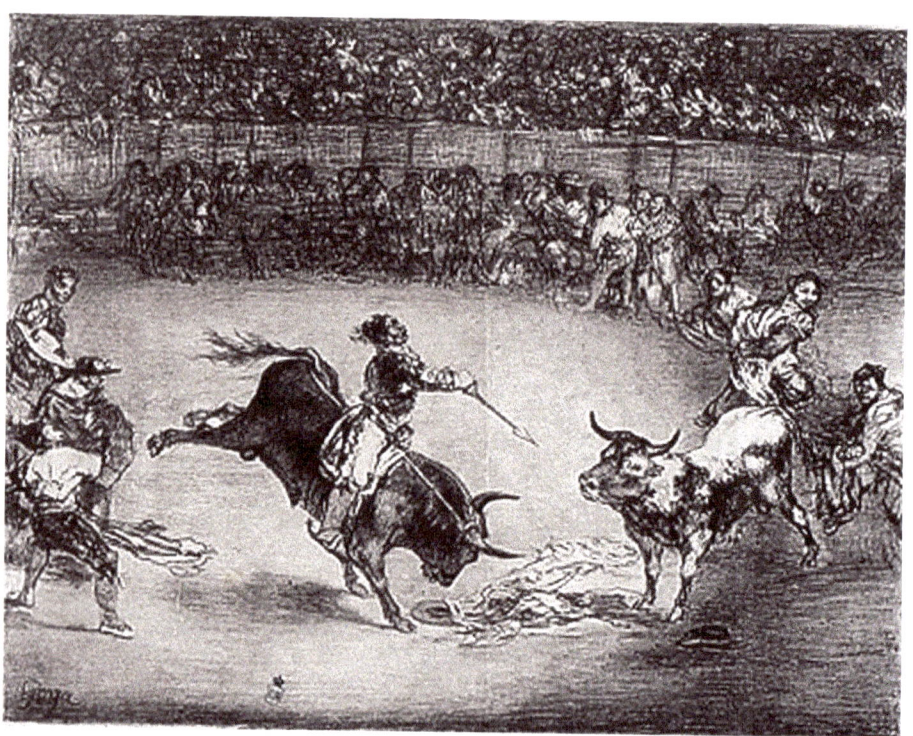

Fun of Spain

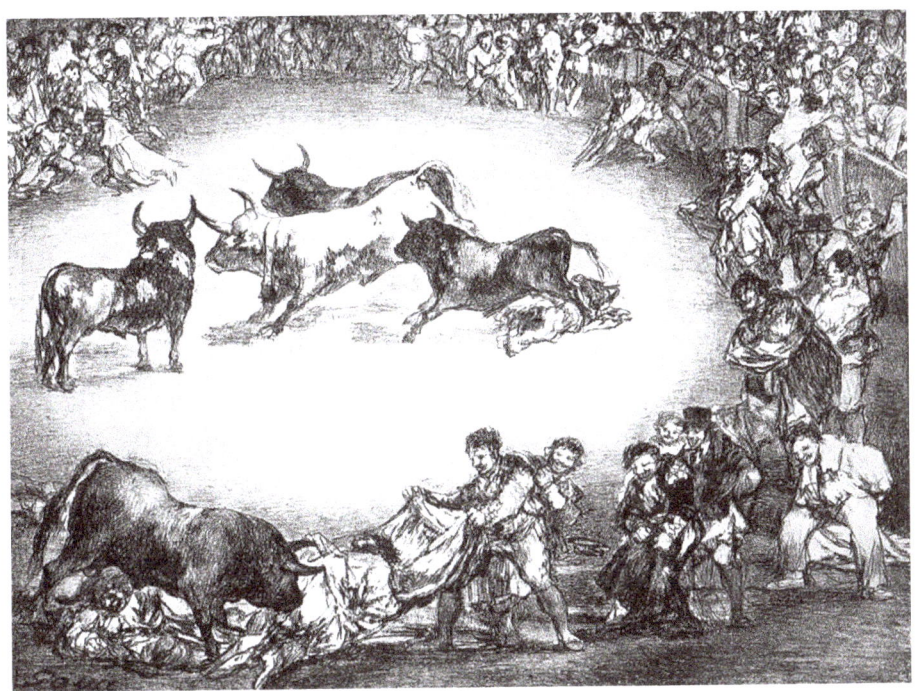

JOSÉ RENÉ CRUZ REVUELTAS

Bordeaux split square

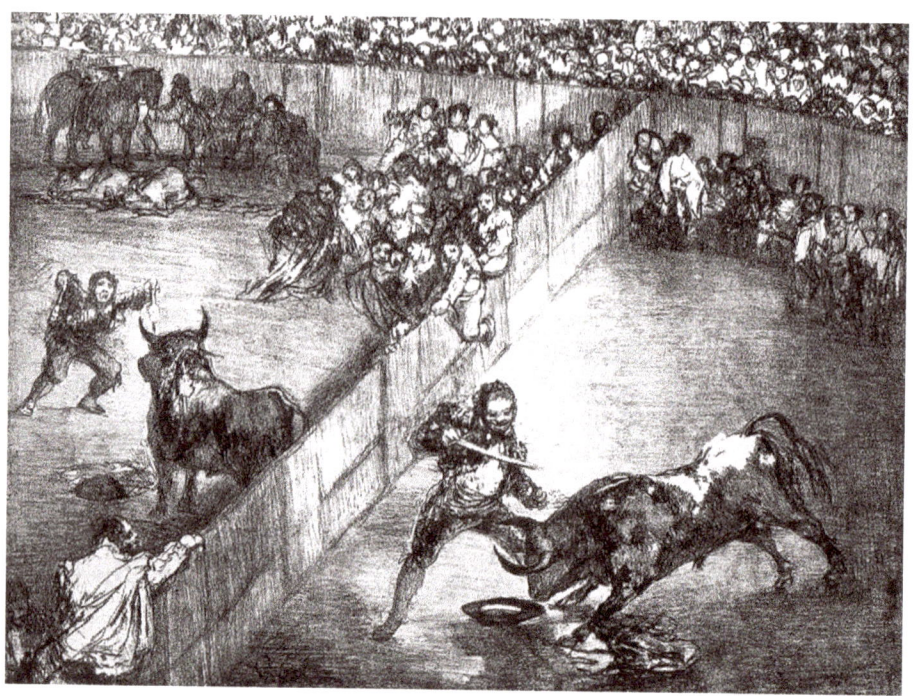

OTHERS

Martincho's recklessness in the plaza de Zaragoza

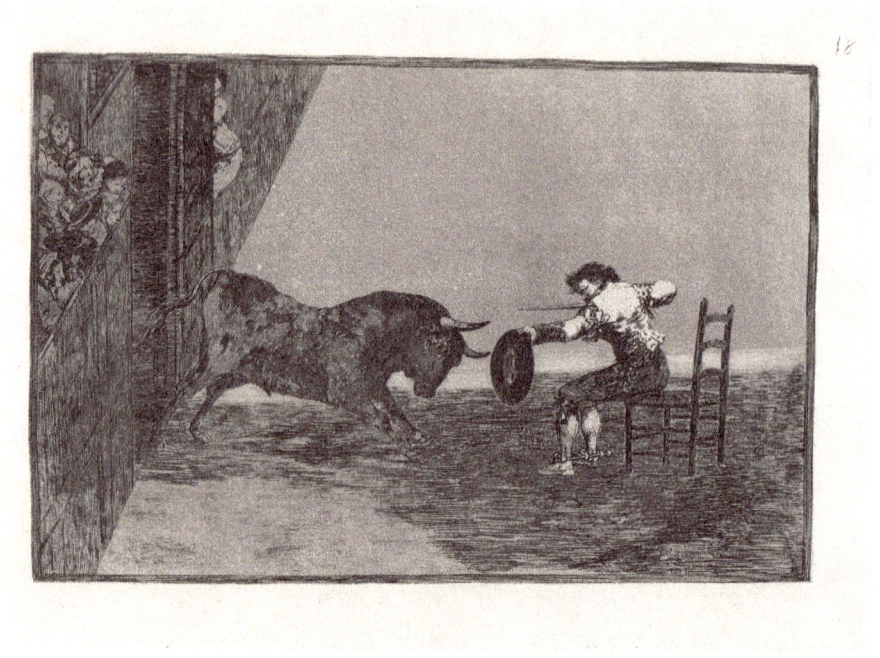

The unfortunate death of Pepe Illo in the square of Madrid

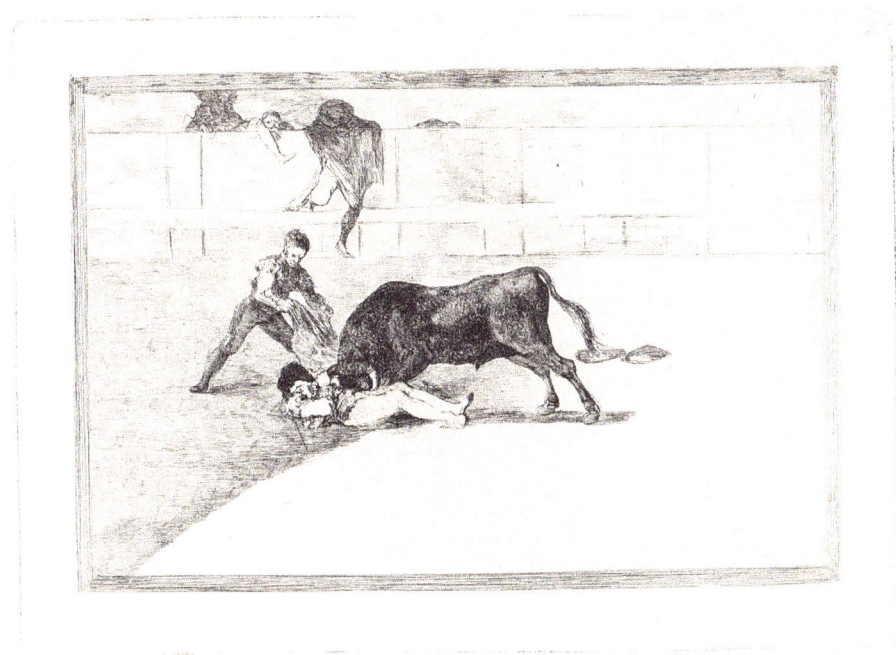

CATALOG OF IDBCOM PUBLISHING

www.idbcom.com
josercrevueltas@idbcom.com

BOOKS IN THIS SERIES

Art

Francisco Of Goya's Engravings: The Caprices, The Disasters Of War, And The Follies

The series of Goya's engravings show us that art does not necessarily have to be beautiful. The monstrous also have a place since it moves us and leads us to feel and reflect; it shows us things as they are but in front of the eyes of our imagination.

Goya titled the series of his engravings, such as The Caprices (1799), The Disasters of War (1815), The Follies (1824), the latter not published until after his death, in the year from 1864.

American Impressionists Volume One: Forty Three Great Artists

Albert Henry Krehbiel, Alson Skinner Clark, Catherine Wiley, Childe Hassam, Colin Campbell Cooper, Daniel Garber, Dennis Miller Bunker, Edmund Charles Tarbell, Edward Charles Volkert, Edward Henry Potthast, Edward Simmons, Edward Willis Redfield, Ernest Lawson, Everett Warner, Frank Weston Benson, Frederick Carl Frieseke, Guy Rose, Henry Bayley Snell, John Henry Twachtman, John Ottis Adams, Joseph Rodefer DeCamp, Julian Alden Weir, Leonard Ochtman.

American Impressionists. Volume Two

Lilla Cabot Perry, Lucy Angeline Bacon, M. Evelyn McCormick, Mary Agnes Yerkes, Mary Cassatt, Otto Stark, Paul Dougherty, Richard E. Miller, Richard Gruelle, Robert Lewis Reid, T. C. Steele, Theodore Earl Butler, Theodore Robinson, Thomas Dewing, Walter Launt Palmer, Willard Leroy Metcalf, William Langson Lathrop, William McGregor Paxton, William Merritt Chase, Wilson Irvine, Theodore Robinson.

Why The War? : The Disasters Of War

During 1931 and 1932, when the winds of World War II were beginning to blow, Albert Einstein, Nobel Laureate in Physics, under the auspices of the International Institute for Intellectual Cooperation, initiated a public debate with the famous psychoanalyst Sigmund Freud on the causes and remedies, of wars. This book presents the response of the psychoanalyst's father.

In addition to "Why War," this book contains "The Disasters of War," one of the most impressive graphic manifestations of war in history.